Lecture Notes in Economics and Mathematical Systems

For information about Vols. 1–49, please contact your bookseller or Springer-Verlag

Vol. 50: Unternehmensforschung Heute – Übersichtsvorträge der Züricher Tagung von SVOR und DGU, September 1970. Herausgegeben von M. Beckmann. IV, 133 Seiten. 1971.

Vol. 51: Digitale Simulation. Herausgegeben von K. Bauknecht und W. Nef. IV, 207 Seiten. 1971.

Vol. 52: Invariant Imbedding. Proceedings 1970. Edited by R. E. Bellman and E. D. Denman. IV, 148 pages. 1971.

Vol. 53: J. Rosenmüller, Kooperative Spiele und Märkte. III, 152 Seiten. 1971.

Vol. 54: C. C. von Weizsäcker, Steady State Capital Theory. III, 102 pages. 1971.

Vol. 55: P. A. V. B. Swamy, Statistical Inference in Random Coefficient Regression Models. VIII, 209 pages. 1971.

Vol. 56: Mohamed A. El-Hodiri, Constrained Extrema. Introduction to the Differentiable Case with Economic Applications. III, 130 pages. 1971.

Vol. 57: E. Freund, Zeitvariable Mehrgrößensysteme. VIII,160 Seiten. 1971.

Vol. 58: P. B. Hagelschuer, Theorie der linearen Dekomposition. VII, 191 Seiten. 1971.

Vol. 59: J. A. Hanson, Growth in Open Economies. V, 128 pages. 1971.

Vol. 60: H. Hauptmann, Schätz- und Kontrolltheorie in stetigen dynamischen Wirtschaftsmodellen. V, 104 Seiten. 1971.

Vol. 61: K. H. F. Meyer, Wartesysteme mit variabler Bearbeitungsrate. VII, 314 Seiten. 1971.

Vol. 62: W. Krelle u. G. Gabisch unter Mitarbeit von J. Burgermeister, Wachstumstheorie. VII, 223 Seiten. 1972.

Vol. 63: J. Kohlas, Monte Carlo Simulation im Operations Research. VI, 162 Seiten. 1972.

Vol. 64: P. Gessner u. K. Spremann, Optimierung in Funktionenräumen. IV, 120 Seiten. 1972.

Vol. 65: W. Everling, Exercises in Computer Systems Analysis. VIII, 184 pages. 1972.

Vol. 66: F. Bauer, P. Garabedian and D. Korn, Supercritical Wing Sections. V, 211 pages. 1972.

Vol. 67: I. V. Girsanov, Lectures on Mathematical Theory of Extremum Problems. V, 136 pages. 1972.

Vol. 68: J. Loeckx, Computability and Decidability. An Introduction for Students of Computer Science. VI, 76 pages. 1972.

Vol. 69: S. Ashour, Sequencing Theory. V, 133 pages. 1972.

Vol. 70: J. P. Brown, The Economic Effects of Floods. Investigations of a Stochastic Model of Rational Investment. Behavior in the Face of Floods. V, 87 pages. 1972.

Vol. 71: R. Henn und O. Opitz, Konsum- und Produktionstheorie II. V, 134 Seiten. 1972.

Vol. 72: T. P. Bagchi and J. G. C. Templeton, Numerical Methods in Markov Chains and Bulk Queues. XI, 89 pages. 1972.

Vol. 73: H. Kiendl, Suboptimale Regler mit abschnittweise linearer Struktur. VI, 146 Seiten. 1972.

Vol. 74: F. Pokropp, Aggregation von Produktionsfunktionen. VI, 107 Seiten. 1972.

Vol. 75: GI-Gesellschaft für Informatik e.V. Bericht Nr. 3. 1. Fachtagung über Programmiersprachen · München, 9.–11. März 1971. Herausgegeben im Auftrag der Gesellschaft für Informatik von H. Langmaack und M. Paul. VII, 280 Seiten. 1972.

Vol. 76: G. Fandel, Optimale Entscheidung bei mehrfacher Zielsetzung. II, 121 Seiten. 1972.

Vol. 77: A. Auslender, Problemes de Minimax via l'Analyse Convexe et les Inégalités Variationelles: Théorie et Algorithmes. VII, 132 pages. 1972.

Vol. 78: GI-Gesellschaft für Informatik e.V. 2. Jahrestagung, Karlsruhe, 2.–4. Oktober 1972. Herausgegeben im Auftrag der Gesellschaft für Informatik von P. Deussen. XI, 576 Seiten. 1973.

Vol. 79: A. Berman, Cones, Matrices and Mathematical Programming. V, 96 pages. 1973.

Vol. 80: International Seminar on Trends in Mathematical Modelling, Venice, 13–18 December 1971. Edited by N. Hawkes. VI, 288 pages. 1973.

Vol. 81: Advanced Course on Software Engineering. Edited by F. L. Bauer. XII, 545 pages. 1973.

Vol. 82: R. Saeks, Resolution Space, Operators and Systems. X, 267 pages. 1973.

Vol. 83: NTG/GI-Gesellschaft für Informatik, Nachrichtentechnische Gesellschaft. Fachtagung „Cognitive Verfahren und Systeme", Hamburg, 11.–13. April 1973. Herausgegeben im Auftrag der NTG/GI von Th. Einsele, W. Giloi und H.-H. Nagel. VIII, 373 Seiten. 1973.

Vol. 84: A. V. Balakrishnan, Stochastic Differential Systems I. Filtering and Control. A Function Space Approach. V, 252 pages. 1973.

Vol. 85: T. Page, Economics of Involuntary Transfers: A Unified Approach to Pollution and Congestion Externalities. XI, 159 pages. 1973.

Vol. 86: Symposium on the Theory of Scheduling and its Applications. Edited by S. E. Elmaghraby. VIII, 437 pages. 1973.

Vol. 87: G. F. Newell, Approximate Stochastic Behavior of n-Server Service Systems with Large n. VII, 118 pages. 1973.

Vol. 88: H. Steckhan, Güterströme in Netzen. VII, 134 Seiten. 1973.

Vol. 89: J. P. Wallace and A. Sherret, Estimation of Product. Attributes and Their Importances. V, 94 pages. 1973.

Vol. 90: J.-F. Richard, Posterior and Predictive Densities for Simultaneous Equation Models. VI, 226 pages. 1973.

Vol. 91: Th. Marschak and R. Selten, General Equilibrium with Price-Making Firms. XI, 246 pages. 1974.

Vol. 92: E. Dierker, Topological Methods in Walrasian Economics. IV, 130 pages. 1974.

Vol. 93: 4th IFAC/IFIP International Conference on Digital Computer Applications to Process Control, Part I. Zürich/Switzerland, March 19–22, 1974. Edited by M. Mansour and W. Schaufelberger. XVIII, 544 pages. 1974.

Vol. 94: 4th IFAC/IFIP International Conference on Digital Computer Applications to Process Control, Part II. Zürich/Switzerland, March 19–22, 1974. Edited by M. Mansour and W. Schaufelberger. XVIII, 546 pages. 1974.

Vol. 95: M. Zeleny, Linear Multiobjective Programming. X, 220 pages. 1974.

Vol. 96: O. Moeschlin, Zur Theorie von Neumannscher Wachstumsmodelle. XI, 115 Seiten. 1974.

Vol. 97: G. Schmidt, Über die Stabilität des einfachen Bedienungskanals. VII, 147 Seiten. 1974.

Vol. 98: Mathematical Methods in Queueing Theory. Proceedings 1973. Edited by A. B. Clarke. VII, 374 pages. 1974.

Vol. 99: Production Theory. Edited by W. Eichhorn, R. Henn, O. Opitz, and R. W. Shephard. VIII, 386 pages. 1974.

Vol. 100: B. S. Duran and P. L. Odell, Cluster Analysis. A Survey. VI, 137 pages. 1974.

continuation on page 169

Lecture Notes
in Economics and
Mathematical Systems

Managing Editors: M. Beckmann and W. Krelle
Economic Theory

207

Y. Fujimori

Modern Analysis of Value Theory

Springer-Verlag Berlin Heidelberg GmbH 1982

Author

Y. Fujimori
Josai University
1-1 Keyakidai, Sakado
Saitama, Japan

ISBN 978-3-540-11949-4 ISBN 978-3-642-45543-8 (eBook)
DOI 10.1007/978-3-642-45543-8

PREFACE

This volume studies the development of Marxian value theory in a modernised context.

The controversy about Marx's value theory is now in its third stage. The first stage was marked by Böhm-Bawerk, and the second by Samuelson soon after the World War II. In this second stage, the basic results in Marx's economics were examined and formulated by Okishio and Morishima-Seton in the Leontief economy case. The third stage was opened by Morishima, who developed the Marxian theory of value on the basis of von Neumann's theory.

In Chapters I through IV, a concise but comprehensive overview of the points in Marx's value theory is presented from the Leontief to von Neumann economy cases.

Based on the above, the two subjects, namely, the reduction of skilled labour and heterogeneous labour and the Marxian theory of differential rent, are developed in Chapters V and VI respectively. These topics, especially the reduction problem, seem not to have been duly discussed in other literature.

The main concern of our discussion, in Chapters I through V in particular, is the so-called fundamental Marxian theorem and the dual dualities, i.e., the duality of price and quantity systems on the basis of the duality of value and price. The author also tried to shed light on superhistorical aspects of Marxian value theory, which ought to give a clue to the insight of the commodity production in general.

The author acknowledges thanks to Professors S.Koshimura, A. Heertje, M.Morishima, D.Furth, Y.Murata, U.Krause and I.Steedman for their encouragement and helpful comments on an earlier draft. Thanks are also due to many friends, although their names are not mentioned here, who have inspired the author through discussion and correspondence. Any remaining errors should, needless to say, be blamed on the author.

July 1982, Tokyo. Y.Fujimori.

GENERAL REMARKS

I. Unless otherwise stated, the following remarks apply.

1. Each chapter should be regarded as an independent entity in the sense that such expressions in the text, as "in what follows," "in the preceding discussion" or the like, should not be extended to the following and preceding chapter(s).
2. Assumptions, once introduced, are supposed to hold throughout the chapter concerned, and are not necessarily mentioned in the statement(s) of theorem(s) explicitly.
3. In stating the corollaries, the conditions required for them are usually omitted, because they are the same with those stated in the preceding theorem(s) or proposition(s) in most cases.
4. Important variables are determined as solutions of equations or inequalities. In order to describe such systems of equations or inequalities, dummy variables are necessary. Nevertheless, the same notation with dummy variables is often expected to represent defined concepts so as to economize on the glossary of notation.
5. When the numbering (in brackets) is attached to systems of equations etc., say (2), each equation of the system is indicated in turn by alphabet as (2a), (2b),..

In the case of a linear programming problem, (*a), (*b) etc. indicate the constraints of the problem.
6. Max {...} and Min {...} describe linear programming problems. Whilst, max {...} and min {...} indicate the magnitudes of scalars maximised or minimised.
7. When a cross-reference to other chapters, say Chapter V, is made, mathematical expressions concerned will be mentioned as Theorem V-II, Proposition V-7, etc., whereas, in the same chapter, the chapter number will not be indicated.

II. Mathematical notation

1. Logical notation

$\exists$	:	there exist(s) ... ,
$\forall$	:	all,
$\Longrightarrow$	:	implies,
$\Longleftrightarrow$	:	is equivalent to,

2. Unless otherwise stated, the following will be applied.

$\mathbb{R}^m$ (${}^m\mathbb{R}$)	:	set of the m-column (row) vectors,
0^n (0_n)	:	n-column (row) zero vector,
1^n (1_n)	:	n-column (row) summation vector,
I	:	identity matrix,
e^i	:	unit vector, i-th component of which is unity,
a_i , $(a)_i$	:	i-th component of vector a ,
A^j	:	j-th column of matrix A ,
$\hat{a}$	:	diagonal matrix composed of vector a ,
${}^tA$	:	transpose of matrix (vector) A ,
$\rho(A)$	:	Frobenius root of matrix A ,
$\Theta(A)$.($\Theta({}^tA)$)	:	right-hand (left-hand) side Frobenius vector of matrix A ,
R(A)	:	space spanned by the column vectors of matrix A ,
A^-	:	generalised inverse of matrix A ,
ε	:	is an element of,
$\mathbb{R}^m_+$, ${}^m\mathbb{R}_+$	:	first quadrant of m-space,
$x > y$	:	$x_i > y_i$ for $\forall$ i,
$x \geq y$	:	$x_i \geqq y_i$ for $\forall$ i, and $\exists$ i such that $x_i > y_i$.
$x \geqq y$	:	$x_i \geqq y_i$ for $\forall$ i .
l.c.m.	:	least common multiple,
card.	:	cardinal number of a set.

3. Major symbols.

A	:	input matrix,
B	:	output matrix,
F	:	wage goods vector (matrix),
L	:	labour vector (matrix),
$M = A + FL$	:	augmented input matrix,
w	:	(M_1-)value vector,
Λ	:	optimum (M_4-) value vector,
p	:	price vector,
x	:	intensity (output) vector,
π	:	profit rate,
g	:	growth rate,
μ	:	the rate of surplus value,
η	:	the rate of surplus labour,

The notation will be modified as the concepts represented undergo generalisation.

The details of the notation will be listed in the text.

TABLE OF CONTENTS

human labour. By definition, it represents the quantitative aspect of labour. On the other hand, labour can be qualitatively different, when exercised in the production of different kinds of goods. The qualitative aspect of labour is called *concrete useful labour*. Labour is the synthesis of the two.

Labour is said to create goods in the sense that they are obtained through labour -- this does not negate the fact that various means of production are necessary: concrete useful labour gives goods their *use-value* or *utility*, and abstract human labour is embodied or crystallised in them as *value*. One unit of labour as abstract human labour creates the same amount of value, irrespective of its concrete useful labour.

In summary, the foundation of the law of value is:

(i) labour as a function of labour-power,
(ii) two basic forms of labour,
(iii) the duality of labour,
(iv) invariance of the amount of value created by a unit of labour.

The relationships among men into which men enter mutually in production through labour, are a fundamental social relation, and since they are based on labour they are expressed in terms of value. Marx's value theory is, based on the above foundation, all about how the relationships among goods are based on the production relationships, and how the latter are transformed into the former.

3. This volume concerns how the law of value functions, or, what amounts to the same thing, the consistency of Marx's value theory. The core of the law of value will be examined in a generalised framework. Since the consistency of Marx's value theory is discussed, the above mentioned foundation of the law of value is accepted.

4. The following analysis is carried out by employing the so-called linear economic model or input-output analysis a la Leontief and von Neumann.

A combination of inputs of a production line or a process is represented by a column vector, whilst a set of quantities common to all types of goods, such as prices and values, is represented by a row vector. Quantities concerning processes and outputs are represented by column vectors, such as intensities of processes. For the sake of convenience, the spaces to which those vectors belong are distinguished as $\mathbf{R}^m$ and ${}^m\mathbf{R}$, where necessary.

5. Unless otherwise stated, the ensuing discussion is subject to the following assumptions:

(# 1) The number of goods and the number of processes are finite.

(# 2) Techniques are linear.

(# 3) Each type of good is produced in a unit period.

(# 4) Each process is of point-input and point-output type.

As for the social conditions,

(# 5) The population of society is resolved into two classes, i.e., the capitalist class and the working class.

(# 6) The workers do not save.

(# 7) Choice in consumption is disregarded.

(# 8) Wages are paid in advance.

Note that in Chapter VI on differential rent (# 1) and (# 2) will be relaxed.

CHAPTER I

MARX'S THEORY OF VALUE, PRICE AND GROWTH IN A LEONTIEF ECONOMY

Introduction

The simplest framework of an economy with linear techniques is the so-called Leontief economy. At the outset, it is necessary to stipulate the framework of a Leontief economy.

An economy satisfying the following conditions:

(F.1) no fixed capital,

(F.2) no alternative techniques,

(F.3) no joint-production,

(F.4) homogeneous labour,

is called a (*simple*) *Leontief economy*.

Consider a Leontief economy producing n types of good. As defined above, this economy has n processes, each producing only one type of good. It is supposed that process i produces good i, and that a unit of operation of process i produces one unit of good i. Then, the output matrix can be represented by I .

Furthermore, let

A n x n : input matrix,

L 1 x n : labour vector,

and the input-output relationships of a Leontief economy can be expressed by

$$\begin{pmatrix} A \\ L \end{pmatrix} \dashrightarrow I .$$

Since the levels of operation of the processes fall with equal magnitudes on their outputs, the two can be identified. In other words, the product space is equivalent to the operation space. In a Leontief economy, process i is also termed *industry* i.

§ 1. The theory of value and surplus value.

1. Let

x $n \times 1$: output vector,

y $n \times 1$: net product vector,

and the excess of the output over input necessary for it defines the *net product*:

(1) $$y = x - Ax \ .$$ [1]

The most fundamental requisite of an economy is that it is productive:

DEFINITION 1.(Productiveness) If it is possible that outputs exceed the amount of inputs used up for their production in an economy, then it is said to be productive: an economy satisfying the productiveness condition

(Pd.C) $$\exists\, x \geqq 0^n : \ x > Ax \ ,$$

is called productive, or simply, A is productive.

It is also possible to consider productiveness in a stronger sense.

DEFINITION 2.(Strong productiveness) An economy is said to be productive in a strong sense if it satisfies the strong productiveness condition,

(S.Pd.C) For $\forall\, y > 0^n, \ \exists\, x \geqq 0^n : x = Ax + y \ .$

That is, in a strongly productive economy, any combination of net products can be produced. Hence, strong productiveness formally implies productiveness. In point of fact, furthermore, the two are equivalent. First, make the following:

(A.1) $$A \geqq 0 \ .$$

PROPOSITION 1. S.Pd.C.<===> Pd.C.<===>

(2) $$(I - A)^{-1} \geqq 0 \ .$$

(As for the proof, refer to Lemma 1.)

The equivalence between the two is one of the remarkable features of the Leontief economy.

Rewriting (1), one has

(3) $$x = Ax + y \ .$$

Consider the dual aspect of this, i.e., the valuation of goods. Marx maintained that products have value based on labour, and gave the following definition:

$$\max \Lambda y = \min Lx \ .$$

Moreover, one has:

COROLLARY. M_1-value is an optimum solution of the above maximizing problem: $\Lambda^o = w$, where Λ^o is a maximizer.

(The proof is easy to show.)

It must be observed here that the equivalence between productiveness and strong productiveness plays an important role.

3. If net products are produced in an economy, the replacement of material inputs is carried out without deficit. Inputs necessary for production comprise , however, labour-power as well as capital goods.

Since labour-power presupposes the existence of a human body, various goods are necessary for the reproduction of labour-power: the means of living required to maintain man's physical condition and the goods necessary for education and/or training of workers. The total value of all these goods consumed by workers enters into the value of labour-power.

The reproduction of labour-power is carried out through consumption, and the consumption goods purchased and consumed by workers are called *wage goods*. Marx wrote:

> "(I)n a given country, at a given period, the average quantity of the means of subsistence necessary for the labourer is practically known."(I, p.171.)

It must be noted that the wage goods bundle of the workers can be presupposed as given like the technical conditions of production. Hence, one may put:

f	$n \times 1$:	standard wage goods bundle,
c	:	the number of units of the standard wage goods bundle,
$F = cf$	:	wage goods bundle per unit of labour.

Make the following assumption:

(A.1^2) $\qquad F \geq 0^n$.

In order for labour-power to be reproduced, the wage goods bundle represented by FLx is necessary for an output vector x . The residue of net products subtracted by this amount of wage goods defines *surplus products*. Let s n x 1 : surplus products vector,

and this is defined by

(7) $$s = x - Ax - FLx \ .$$

For the sake of brevity, write

(8) $$M = A + FL \ ,$$

and (7) is rewritten as

$$s = (I-M)x \ .$$

Thus, the socially aggregated product resolves itself into three parts: physical and material inputs, wage goods and surplus products. Since the values of goods are known, it is possible to measure and aggregate them in terms of value.

Physical inputs and wage goods necessary for capitalist production are called respectively *constant capital* and *variable capital*. The amount of surplus products in terms of value is called *surplus value*.

With respect to industry i, let

$C_i = wa^i x_i$: value of constant capital,

$V_i = wFL_i x_i$: value of variable capital,

and, with respect to the economy as a whole,

$C = \sum C_i$: socially aggregated constant capital,

$V = \sum V_i$: socially aggregated variable capital,

$S = ws$: socially aggregated surplus value.

The ratio of constant capital to variable capital in terms of value is called the value-composition of capital. It is often referred to conventionally as the *organic composition of capital* in the following discussion:

$\xi_i = C_i / V_i$: organic composition of capital in industry i,

$\xi = C / V$: social organic composition of capital.

(Where it is necessary, their dependence on aggregators, such as w and x, will be made explicit.)

Now, the factors of production are physical inputs and labour, but physical inputs and labour-power manifest themselves as the factors of production, because labour is the use-value of labour-power. Hence, it becomes necessary to measure the difference between the value of labour-power and the value created by labour, which represents surplus. Four types of surplus-ratio will be considered according to Marx's definitions.

DEFINITION 5. (The rate of surplus value) The rate of surplus value is the ratio of surplus value to variable capital.

Let

μ : rate of surplus value,

and this is expressed by

(9) $$\mu = \frac{S}{V} .$$

The concept of surplus value can be grasped from the angle of the social expenditure of labour.

DEFINITION 6. (Necessary labour) An amount of labour required to produce the wage goods bundles for the workers is called necessary labour.

Let

$\bar{x}$ n x 1 : necessary output vector,

which satisfies

(10) $$\bar{x} = A\bar{x} + FLx ,$$

for a given output vector x, and $L\bar{x}$ represents necessary labour.

DEFINITION 7. (Surplus labour) The residue of total labour subtracted by necessary labour defines surplus labour. Namely, $Lx - L\bar{x}$.

From the above, one can define:

DEFINITION 8. (The rate of surplus labour) The rate of surplus labour is the ratio of surplus labour to necessary labour.

Let

η : rate of surplus labour,

and this is determined by

(11) $$\eta = \frac{Lx - L\bar{x}}{L\bar{x}} .$$

Since the amount of labour laid out is not equal to the value of wage goods, it is also possible to divide labour into two portions: the one wages are paid for, and the other not. The part of labour for which wages are paid is termed *paid labour*, and the rest *unpaid labour.* The magnitudes of the two are evaluated as follows: let

N : the number of workers,

T : workday (e.g., hours),

F* n x 1: wage goods bundle per workday.

Without loss of generality, one can presuppose that one hour of labour expenditure measures one unit of labour, so that one has

(12) $$TN = Lx \ .$$

Since a worker receives wF^* per workday, wF^* expresses paid labour, whilst $T - wF^*$ represents unpaid labour. Then, the *rate of unpaid labour to paid labour*, the third surplus-ratio, is defined by:

(13) $$\mu' = \frac{T - wF^*}{wF^*} \ .$$

It is also seen that the relationship between F and F^* is given by

(14) $$\frac{1}{T}F^* = F \ .$$

That is, one may put $F^* = f$ and $1/T = c$.

If the workday of a worker is divided into two portions, i.e., the one for himself T' , *necessary working-time*, and the other for capitalists, $T - T'$, *surplus working-time*, one has

(15) $$T'N = wF^*N \ ,$$

for all workers. Then, the *rate of surplus working-time* can be defined by

(16) $$\mu'' = \frac{TN - T'N}{T'N} \ .$$

The rates introduced above are called the rates of surplus, all representing the rate of exploitation in the capitalist economy. The first point to be discussed with respect to them is their equivalence.

THEOREM II. The rate of surplus value is equal to the rate of surplus labour: $\mu = \eta$.

Proof.

Evaluate necessary labour, and one has

$$L\bar{x} = L(I-A)^{-1}FLx$$
$$= wFLx \ .$$

Hence, it follows that

$$\eta = \frac{Lx - wFLx}{wFLx} \; ,$$

whilst, in the light of Proposition 3, the rate of surplus value is evaluated as

$$\mu = \frac{w(I-M)x}{wFLx} = \frac{Lx - wFLx}{wFLx} \; .$$

Hence, $\mu = \eta$. Q.E.D.

COROLLARY 1. $\mu' = \eta$.

In fact, from (13), it follows that

$$\mu' = \frac{1}{wF} - 1 = \frac{Lx}{wFLx} - 1 = \eta \; .$$

COROLLARY 2. $\mu'' = \eta$.

In fact, substitute (12) and (15) into (16), and the result is soon obtained.

It has been made clear that the rate of surplus value can be defined as the ratio of surplus value created by a unit of labour to the value of labour-power of one unit:

(17) $$\mu = \frac{1}{wF} - 1 \; .$$

Since the wage goods bundle is given, the rate of surplus value takes a uniform magnitude in all the industries.

4. It is now established that the four types of surplus are all equivalent. The most important among them will be the rates of surplus value and surplus labour. The equivalence of the two rates is derived from the fact that the productiveness of the economy ensures the existence of M_1-value and its equality to M_2-value. In fact, if one examines the evaluation of necessary labour, one has

$$L\bar{x} = L_1\bar{x}_1 + \cdots + L_n\bar{x}_n$$

$$= w_1^*\bar{y}_1 + \cdots + w_n^*\bar{y}_n \; ,$$

where $\bar{y} = (I-A)\bar{x}$.

It should be recognised that the amount of necessary labour, and hence the rate of surplus labour, can be evaluated independently of the value equation. The rate of surplus labour is instead related to M_2-value, if one were to relate it to the value of individual goods.

At the same time, the rate of surplus value depends on the value equation and hence M_1-value: without knowing M_1-value of goods, one cannot evaluate it.

Nevertheless, the rate of surplus value is equal to the rate of surplus labour (Theorem II), because in a Leontief economy the solvability of the value equation is equivalent to the productiveness of the economy (Proposition 3), and the amount of net products in terms of value is equal to the amount of labour laid out (Proposition 2), and M_1-value is equivalent to M_2-value (Theorem I).

To reconfirm this point seems very important in generalising Marx's economics in the subsequent chapters.

5. Since the wage goods bundle is given, the level of the rate of surplus value can be determined in practical terms.

The amount of labour expended is, as expressed in (12), equal to the number of the workers multiplied by the length of the workday, so that changes in the length of the workday bring about changes in the amount of labour. The rate of surplus value thus undergoes alteration as the length of the workday varies. In fact, one has

$$\mu = \frac{T - wF^*}{wF^*} = \frac{1 - w\left(\frac{1}{T}\right)F^*}{w\left(\frac{1}{T}\right)F^*},$$

where it is seen that a worker receives $1/T$ units of wage goods bundle per hour. $1/T$ represents the real wage rate, which is inversely related to the length of the workday.

The rate of surplus value as a function of the real wage rate, $\mu = \mu(1/T)$, is a decreasing function. Its domain is determined by the physical, cultural and social bounds, on one side, and the value of labour-power on the other. That is, the length of the workday should satisfy

$$wF^* \leqq T \leqq T^M,$$

where T^M indicates the physical, cultural and social bounds. Thus, the domain is represented by $(1/T^M, 1/wF^*)$.

§ 2. The fundamental Marxian theorem.

1. In the economic system in which the capitalist mode of production is pervasive, products are not exchanged at their values.

Once labour-power has been purchased by capital, it is united with the means of production, and the use-value of labour-power, i.e., labour is embodied in capital. The productivity of labour becomes part of the productivity of capital, and the results of production are appropriated by capital as products of capital.

That the source of profit is surplus value is the most important point of Marx's economics, and this is termed precisely the fundamental Marxian theorem. Marx, however, did not demonstrate this theorem rigorously. The aim of this section is to make a rigorous and analytical discussion of the theorem.

First, consider the following definition:

DEFINITION 9.(Reproducibility) An economy which can produce surplus products in all industries is called reproducible: an economy fulfilling the subsequent surplus condition,

(S.C.) $\exists\, x \geqq 0^m:\ x \geq Mx$,

is said to be reproducible.[3)]

It is trivial that a reproducible economy is productive.

In the next place, consider the dual aspect of reproducibility. Given a valuation vector of products, p . For it, pA and pFL represent physical costs and wages per unit of products in industries, so that pM expresses total costs per unit of products. The residue of unit valuation subtracted by total cost is called *profit*. Let

p 1 x n : valuation vector,
Π 1 x n : profit vector,

and, they satisfy

(18) $\Pi = p - pM$.

DEFINITION 10.(Profitability) An economy which can produce profit in the industries for a given valuation vector is called profitable: an economy fulfilling the following profitability condition,

(Pf.C) $\exists\, p \geq 0_n:\ p > pM$,

is called profitable.

One immediately obtains:

THEOREM III. (Fundamental duality) Reproducibility is equivalent to profitability: S.C. <===> Pf.C.

Proof.

In fact, it is easy to see that both are equivalent to

$$(I-M)^{-1} \geqq 0 \ . \qquad \text{Q.E.D.}$$

That is, if surplus products are producible in all the industries in a Leontief economy, profit is possible in the economy, and vice-versa. What is significant here is that profitability is derived from reproducibility independently of the concept of value. A very strong duality is thus observed in a Leontief economy.

As an immediate corollary of the above, one has the relationship between profitability and positivity of the rate of surplus value:

THEOREM IV. (Fundamental Marxian theorem) An economy is profitable if and only if the rate of surplus value is positive and there exists a positive value: Pf.C. $\Longleftrightarrow$ $\mu > o$ and $\exists\, w > 0_n$.

Proof.

From Theorem III, Pf.C. implies $(I-M)^{-1} \geqq 0$, and hence Pd.C. From Proposition 2, one has $w = L(I-A)^{-1} > 0_n$.

Now, if $wF \geq 1$, then one has

$$w = wA + L \leq wA + wFL = wM \ ,$$

which contradicts $(I-M)^{-1} \geqq 0$.

Conversely, if $\mu > o$ and $\exists w > 0_n$ is true, then $(1+\mu)wF = 1$ from (17), so that rewriting (4) gives

$$w = wA + (1+\mu)wFL > w(A+FL) \ .$$

Hence, Pf.C. follows. Q.E.D.

The Marxian interpretation of this theorem is that the source of profit is surplus value. Namely, surplus value created by labour is appropriated by capital as profit: capital exploits labour. This explains the most significant qualitative feature of the capitalist economy that profit is the transformed form of surplus value.

Then, how does this transformation take place? This will be discussed in the next section.

§ 3. Theory of transformation.

1. Competition among capitalists pursuing a greater amount of profit equalises the rates of profit over capital in all production lines. Accordingly, valuations of products, or prices of goods at which they are exchanged, should not only guarantee positive profit, but also bring about an equal rate of profit.[4)]

As mentioned before, the creativeness of labour appears as part of the productivity of capital. Through the commoditization of labour-power, capital can appropriate the productivity of labour at the wage level, so that profit, as the fruits of production, appears as the products of material inputs and wages, i.e., constant and variable capital. Consequently, the rate of profit over total capital measures its efficiency.

In the state of the economy with an equal rate of profit, the efficiency of capital is equal in all production lines, and the economy is in equilibrium in the sense that no further transference of capital from one production sphere to another for a higher profit rate is motivated. Valuations of goods corresponding to such an equal profit rate are designated as *production prices* by Marx.[5)]

The purpose of this section is to summarize Marx's theory of transformation from values to production prices.

2. A formal definition of equilibrium profitability is expressed as *DEFINITION 11.(Equilibrium profitability)* Prices at which all production processes can attain an equal rate of profit are called equilibrium profitable.

That is, let

π : equilibrium profit rate,

p $1 \times n$: production price vector,

and prices satisfying the subsequent condition:

(E.Pf.C) $\exists\ \pi > o\ ,\ p \geq 0_n$, such that

(19) $$p = (1+\pi)pM\ ,$$ [6)]

are called equilibrium profitable.

It is trivial that E.Pf.C. implies Pf.C. In a Leontief economy, however, the converse is also true.

PROPOSITION 4. Equilibrium profitability is equivalent to profitability: E.Pf.C.<===> Pf.C.

Proof.

The "==>" part is formal, so that one has only to show the "==>" part. In fact, if $p > 0_n$ and $p > pM$, then there exist a positive eigenvalue of M and a nonnegative eigen-vector associated with it such that

$$o < \rho(M) < 1 \, ,$$
$$\rho(M)\cdot\theta({}^tM) = \theta({}^tM)M \, . \qquad \text{Q.E.D.}$$

As shown in the above proof, the profit rate and the production prices are uniquely determined by the Frobenius root and the Frobenius vector of the matrix M :

(20)
$$\pi = \frac{1}{\rho(M)} - 1 \, ,$$
$$p = \theta({}^tM) \, .$$

According to the above determination of the profit rate and the production prices, they are solely dependent, in appearance, on A , L , and F : is the production price system (19) regulated by the value system? If it is so, in what sense? This issue must be discussed.

3. In *Capital* III, Marx developed a procedure to evaluate the rate of profit and the production prices in terms of value. His original procedure can be sketched as follows.

Assume that products are sold at their values and that profit is equal to surplus value. Define

cost price = constant capital + variable capital ,

and one has

value = cost price + surplus value .[7)]

Aggregate the values of goods, and find the ratio of surplus value to cost price, which defines the profit rate. By multiplying cost-price by 1+profit rate, one has the production prices of products.

Putting the above procedure in mathematical notation, one has, as the profit rate,

$$\pi^o = \frac{\mu wFLx}{w(A+FL)x} \, ,$$

for an output vector x . Evidently, one gets

(21)
$$\pi^o = \frac{\mu}{1 + \xi} \, .$$

Namely, the profit rate "approximately" defined by Marx is the rate of surplus value divided by 1 + organic composition of capital.

Marx expressed the production price system as

$$(22) \qquad w^1 = (1+\pi^o)w(A + FL) \ .$$

The inequality $\mu > \pi^o$ as well as (21) and (22) constitute Marx's transformation theorem (I).

It must be noted, however, that this iteration procedure was not completed by Marx: since prices are obtained by (22), cost price (wM) should be reevaluated by those prices, so that the iteration should be repeated ad infinitum. Marx himself was aware of this, but he did not carry out the iteration ad infinitum. The incompleteness of Marx's original treatment is one of the greatest causes of the controversies on the transformation problem.

At the outset, one can show:

PROPOSITION 5. $\mu > o \Longrightarrow \mu > \pi$.

Proof.

Rewriting (4) in view of $\mu > o$, one has

$$w = wA + (1+\mu)wFL < (1+\mu)wM \ .$$

In the light of Lemma 5(iv), one has

$$\frac{1}{1+\mu} > \rho(M) \ .$$

Hence, in view of (20a), one obtains the conclusion. Q.E.D.

Namely, if the rate of surplus value is positive, it is greater than the profit rate.

In the next stage, the convergence of the transformation of values (4) into prices (19) was rigorously proved by Okishio (4).

In a general iteration formula, Marx's procedure can be represented by the sequences $\{w^t\}$ and $\{\pi^t\}$ defined as, for $x \geq 0^n$,

$$w^{t+1} = (1+\pi^t)w^t \cdot M \ ,$$

$$(23) \qquad 1+\pi^t = \frac{w^t \cdot x}{w^t \cdot Mx} \ ,$$

$$w^o = w \ .$$

Then,

PROPOSITION 6. Assume M is stable. The sequences, $\{w^t\}$ and $\{\pi^t\}$, generated by (23), converge:

$$\lim_{t\to\infty} w^t = p^* \ , \ \lim_{t\to\infty} \pi^t = \frac{1}{\rho(M)} - 1 \ ,$$

where, p^* satisfies (19) and,

(24) $$p^*x = wx \ .$$

(As for the proof, refer to Okishio [4]. Also see Chapter III.)

Namely, if Marx's procedure is iterated ad infinitum, the value system is transformed into the production price system. Moreover, as shown by (24), the production price as the limit of the transformation has the same dimension with value, and normalization is made in the sense that for any output vector the total price of that output is equal to its total value. Here, the total value plays the role of numeraire.

Accordingly, it is seen that the production price system is completely determined by (19) and (24). In the following discussion, the price vector p^*, normalized as above, is called the (*absolute*) production price.

Marx's transformation theorem (II) concerns the simultaneous establishment of two famous equalities:

total price = total value,

total profit = total surplus value.

These two equalities, however, do not hold simultaneously.

On the basis of Proposition 6, one can write the value and price systems, and the above two equalities:

(4) $$w = wA + L \ ,$$

(19) $$p^* = (1+\pi)p^*M \ ,$$

(25) $$p^*x = wx \ ,$$

(26) $$p^*(I-M)x = w(I-M)x \ .$$

From the angle of determining the production prices and the profit rate, equation (4) is independent and closed, so that it can be excluded. The remaining equations, (19), (25) and (26), give $n+2$ equations in $n+1$ unknowns: they are overdetermined. Therefore, two of the equalities do not hold simultaneously. The subsequent proposition gives a clue to understanding this.

PROPOSITION 7. If any two of the following are true:

total price = total value,

total profit = total surplus value,

total cost price = total cost-value,

then the remaining equality is also true.

(The proof is trivial.)

Even if the first equality, total price = total value, for instance, is presupposed, the second equality, total profit = total surplus value, does not follow immediately, because the total cost-price deviates from the total cost-value. A conjecture may be made that the proportion of outputs, x , and the proportion of direct and indirect inputs, Mx , do not satisfy a certain condition. This point will be discussed in the next subsection.

With attention focused on (25), its implication will be found in the fact that the total amount of products realised in the market takes a magnitude independent of the conditions in the market.

4. Consider, as before, the dual aspect of the production price system (19). Suppose that capitalists expend all their profit to attain the greatest possible growth, and that all production lines are expanding at an equal rate. Such a state of the economy is called *capacity growth*, or *von Neumann growth*. Let

g^c : capacity growth rate (von Neumann growth rate),

x^c $n \times 1$: capacity output vector (von Neumann proportion),

and these two are determined by the capacity growth equation:[8)]

$$x^c = (1+g^c)Mx^c \quad . \tag{27}$$

As is well-known, (19) and (25) define the von Neumann equilibrium (π, p, g^c, x^c). As for the von Neumann equilibrium in a Leontief economy, one has:

PROPOSITION 8. $\pi = g^c$.

In fact, $\pi = g^c = (1/\rho(M)) - 1$.

This shows that g^c is the greatest uniform rate of growth, and that x^c is the output vector associated with it.

In the von Neumann equilibrium, Marx's transformation theorems (I) and (II) can be resurrected as follows:

THEOREM V. (Morishima-Seton's equality) (i)

$$\pi = \frac{\mu}{\xi(x^c)+1} \quad . \tag{28}$$

where $\xi(x^c)$ indicates the dependence of ξ on x^c.

(ii) The following two are equivalent:

$$\begin{aligned} p^*x^c &= wx^c, \\ p^*(I-M)x^c &= w(I-M)x^c. \end{aligned} \tag{29}$$

Proof.

(i) Postmultiply (4) by x^c and premultiply (27) by w, and the following holds:

$$wAx^c + Lx^c = (1+g^c)wMx^c ,$$

from which one can derive

$$g^c = \frac{(1-wF)Lx^c}{wAx^c+wFLx^c} .$$

In the light of the definition of ξ, (17) and Proposition 8, the conclusion follows.

(ii) From (4), (19), (27) and (29a), one can show (29b). In fact, from (4) and (27), it follows that

$$wx^c = (1+g^c)wMx^c .$$

Postmultiply (19) by x^c, and one has

$$p^*x^c = wx^c = (1+\pi)p^*Mx^c ,$$

in view of (29a). By dint of Proposition 8, (29b) follows.

Likewise, by assuming (29b), one can derive (29a). Q.E.D.

Thus, in von Neumann equilibrium the price system is seen to be immediately related to the value system as represented by (28), which is an extension of Marx's original formula of the profit rate, (21).

Now, the quantitative regulation of price by value should be summarized as follows: first, Marx-Okishio's transformation formulae converge, yielding Marx's first transformational equality, and, secondly, in von Neumann equilibrium the profit rate can be evaluated in value terms, so that Marx's two transformational equalities are equivalent.

The production of *luxury goods*, which are goods neither directly nor indirectly employed in production, does not enter into the von Neumann proportion.

In fact, without loss of generality, the economy can be divided into two departments: the luxury goods producing department II and the non-luxury goods producing department I. The matrix M can be partioned into

(30) $$M = \begin{pmatrix} M_I & M_{II} \\ 0 & 0 \end{pmatrix} .$$

Let the von Neumann proportion determined by (27) be partitioned, in the same way as (30),

$$x^c = \begin{pmatrix} x_I^c \\ x_{II}^c \end{pmatrix} ,$$

and it is easy to see that

$$x^c_{II} = 0^k ,$$

where the last k types of good are luxury goods.

Therefore, the actual output is different from the von Neumann proportion in general. Nevertheless, Morishima-Seton's equality can be generalised as follows. Let us define:

DEFINITION 11.(Greatest equilibrium growth rate) For $x \in \mathbb{R}^n$,

$$g^M(x) = \max \{g \mid x \geq (1+g)Mx .\}$$

Then, one can show:

PROPOSITION 9.(Growth constraint)

(32) $$g^M(x) < \frac{\mu}{1+\xi(x)} .$$

Proof.

Premultiplying (31) by w , one has

$$g^M(x)wMx \leqq wx - wMx .$$

In the light of the definition of ξ and μ , (32) follows. Q.E.D.

The right-hand side of (32) represents the value rate of profit, so that (32) shows that the greatest equilibrium growth rate cannot exceed the value rate of profit. Namely, growth is constrained in the value dimension. Note that (32) is a generalised formula subsuming (28), as seen from Proposition 8 and Theorem V. Thus, *dual dualities* of value, price and growth are seen to hold in Marx's economics.

With reference to the above Marxian discussion of value, price and growth, it may be relevant to point out the nature of von Neumann equilibrium.

At the outset, let us define two regions:

DEFINITION 12.(Growth region) A set of (output) vectors for which surplus products are possible is called the growth region:

$$\mathbb{P}(M) = \{x \mid x > Mx, x \geq 0^n .\}$$

DEFINITION 13.(Profitable region) A set of price vectors at which profit accrues is called the profitable region:

$$\mathbb{P}^*(M) = \{p \mid p > pM, p \geq 0_n .\}$$

The two are polyhedral cones, whilst the von Neumann equilibrium with a positive von Neumann growth rate and a positive profit rate is represented by half lines in $\mathbb{R}^n_+$ and $^n\mathbb{R}_+$, each representing the von Neumann proportion and production price respectively.

Now, as shown by Theorem III and Proposition 4, the growth region and/or the profitable region are not empty, if and only if there exist such half lines in $\mathbb{R}^n_+$ and $^n\mathbb{R}_+$. In other words, the existence of the von Neumann equilibrium with a positive von Neumann growth rate and a positive profit rate concerns only the possibility of growth and profitability of the economy. In this respect, von Neumann equilibrium is rather a qualitative concept.

Let us note that the fundamental Marxian theorem presents an equivalent condition for the nonemptiness of the two regions, and that this nonemptiness does not depend on the market.

It is also important to note that the nonemptiness of the profitable region is instead a basis for establishing (temporary) equilibrium in the market, because the market itself does not explain why it can establish equilibrium, though it does explain how. Whether or not profit rates are equalised, the actual transactions are carried out in the market: if profit never accrues to some capitalists who are maximising the profit rate, one cannot say that the market functions properly. Thus, it is seen that the nonemptiness of the profitable region is necessary for the market to function normally.

It must be noted, however, that the fundamental Marxian theorem gives no clue to the functions of the market themselves at all. It ensures nothing beyond the possibility. In this sense, the fundamental Marxian theorem is basic, but normative.

5. In addition to the above, Marx put forward other transformation theorems: he maintained, i) that the cost price of a commodity is always smaller than its value, and ii) that the value of a commodity produced by capital with a higher (lower) organic composition of capital is smaller (greater) than its production price, and iii) if the organic composition of certain capital is equal to the social average, the value of a commodity produced by that capital is equal to its production price.

Those propositions discussed by Marx are not, however, easy to show in general terms.

The conditions under which Marx's numerical examples concerning (21) and (22) give the true result have been examined by Morishima [4] in

PROPOSITION 11. In a Marx-Leontief economy, the following hold:
(i) (34) implies (37).
(ii)(33) implies (37).
(iii)(39)<===> $\pi^o = \pi$, $w^1 = p$ in (20), (21) and (22).
(As for the proof, see Morishima (4), pp.77-9.)

According to this specialised proposition, (37) comprises the second and third cases pointed out in the preceding subsection, and is a sufficient and necessary condition to justify Marx's original procedure of transformation described by (21) and (22).

The concept of the linear dependence of industries was further generalised by Morishima: industries are said to be of linear dependence of degree h, if

$$\bar{\pi} w(A+FL)\cdot M^{*h} = w(I-M)\cdot M^{*h}, \tag{38}$$

where $M^* = (1+\bar{\pi})M$, and $\bar{\pi} = \dfrac{w(I-M)x^c}{w(A+FL)x^c}$.

The linear dependence of industries is the case of $h = 1$ in (38).
PROPOSITION 12. In a Marx Leontief economy, the industries are linearly dependent at degree h, if and only if the sequence of the production price generated by (23) converges to its limit in finite times h: (38) $\Longleftrightarrow$ $w^h = w^{h+1} = \cdots = p^*$ in (23).
(As for the proof, see Morishima (5), pp.622-32, or Morishima-Catephores, pp.170-1.)

Our comment to be made on Morishima's discussion is that his proposition is valid only in Marx-Leontief economies: the concept of linearly dependent industries is characteristic of the Marx-Leontief economy. (34) does not necessarily imply (38) in the Leontief economy case.[9]

7. An antagonistic relationship between wages and profit has been one of the most important issues in the history of economics. This has already been discussed in the camp of non-Marxian economics, and fundamental results have been obtained. In this subsection, a short note on the rate of surplus value and the wage-profit curve will be made.

In view of $F = cf$, the production price system can be written as

$$p = (1+\pi)p(A+cfL),$$

whilst, the rate of surplus value is expressed as

(39) $$\mu = \frac{1}{cwf} - 1 ,$$

from (17). Then,

PROPOSITION 13. The profit rate is an increasing function of the rate of surplus value:

(40) $$\frac{d\pi}{d\mu} > o .$$

Proof.

In the light of (A.3), one has

(41) $$\frac{d\pi}{dc} < o ,$$

because π is a continuous function of c ; whereas, from (39),

$$\frac{d\mu}{dc} < o$$

is obtained. Hence, the conclusion soon follows. Q.E.D.

§ 4. Conclusions -- Criticism and defence.

1. In the preceding three sections, a modernized overview of Marx's labour theory of value has been provided. By way of summary, the gist of the discussion will be repeated, and an examination of the criticism and a defence will be made.

Two definitions of value introduced by Marx, M_1-value and M_2-value, are equivalent to each other in a Leontief economy, because their existence is reduced to the productiveness of the economy.

Likewise, the reproducibility of the economy is equivalent to its profitability, which is termed the fundamental duality. It should be emphasized that the fundamental duality appears to be independent of the concept of value in the Leontief economy.

The rates of surplus value and surplus labour also coincide with each other owing to the first equivalence of M_1-value and M_2-value. The rate of surplus labour, however, does not necessarily depend on the individual values of products.

On the basis of the above two types of equivalence, the fundamental Marxian theorem is established in terms of the rate of surplus value and surplus labour. It explicates the social source of profit, and hence it is qualitative.

The theory of transformation concerns the evaluation of the profit rate and the levels of price and profit, so that it is quantitative. The theory of transformation is seen to consist of two components -- the transformation of the rate of surplus value into the profit rate, and the equality of total price and total profit to total value and total surplus value respectively. The first transformation can be said to be a quantitative aspect of the fundamental Marxian theorem, because it concerns the newly created value-portion. As shown by Propositions 5 - 9 and Theorem V, the regulation of price by value is straightforwardly observed in the von Neumann equilibrium of a Leontief economy. It must be remarked that one of Marx's transformational equalities, such as total price = total value, mirrors his basic idea that the total price of the products produced in society is independent of the market.

DIAGRAM I-1.

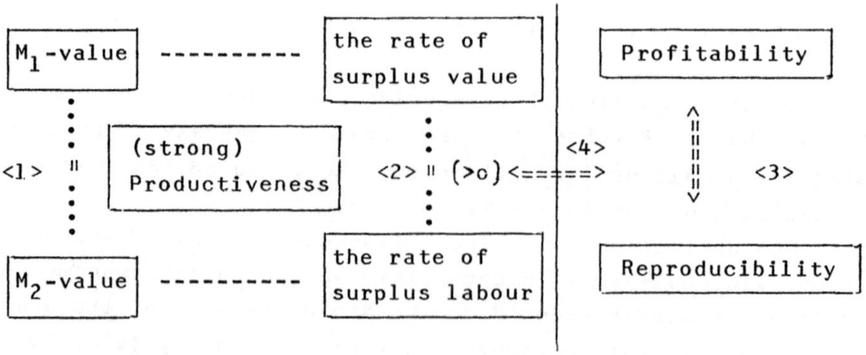

where, <1> Theorem I, <2> Theorem II, <3> Theorem III, <4> Theorem IV.

The synthesis of the qualitative and quantitative thoeories constitutes the major part of Marx's theory of value. The regulation of price by value, or the law of value, should be understood in such a way that it contains the fact stated by the fundamental Marxian theorem. The above diagram illustrates the logical structure of the qualitative aspect of Marx's theory of value.

2. Let us examine the criticism of Marx so far made. Let us begin with Steedman's criticism of Marx.

Steedman examined the equation (19):

$$p = (1+\pi)p(A + FL) ,$$

and concluded that given technical data A , L and the wage goods bundle F , the profit rate π and the production price p are determined independently of values. Namely, the principal conclusion of his criticism of Marx is represnted by the following diagram: (Steedman(4), p.48.)

DIAGRAM I-2.

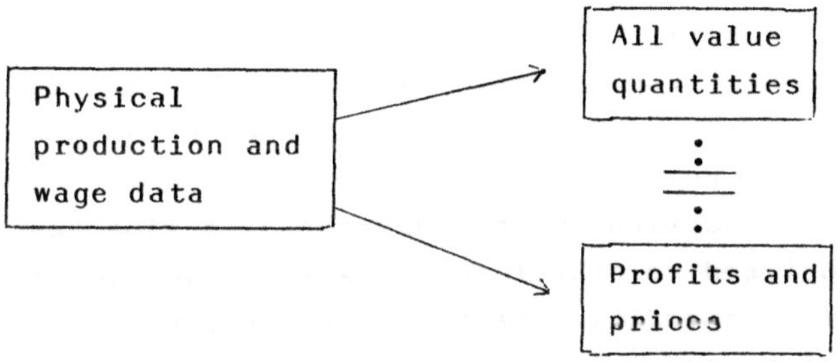

According to Steedman, there is no immediate linkage between the price and value systems: there is no problem called the "transformation problem" at all. Hence, the theory of value is redundant in economics.

In addition to the above, it is relevant to mention that Samuelson criticised Marx because prices are not proportional to values. In fact, Marx maintained that value regulates price in the sense that both prices and values fall or rise in the same direction.(III,p.177) This notion is grasped as the proportionality of prices and values in most literature. It is interesting to note that not only Samuelson but the fruits of capital. Value and surplus value are transformed into prices and profit respectively, and hence unequal exchange into equal exchange.

As regards the importance of the transformation and the fundamental Marxian theorem, Morishima(4) summarized as follows:

> "(T)he transformation problem has the aim of showing how 'the aggregate exploitation of labour on the part of the total social capital' is, in a capitalist economy, obscured by the distortion of prices from values; the other aim is to show how living labour can be the sole source of profit." (Morishima(4), p.86.)

With reference to the social source of profit, Baumol also maintained:

> "The point of the value theory may then be summed up as follows: goods are indeed produced by labour and natural resources together. But the relevant *social* source of production is labour, not an inanimate 'land'. Thus, profits, interest and rent must also be attributed to labour, and their total is equal (tautologically) to the total value produced by labour minus the amount consumed by labour itself. The competitive process, that appears to show that land is the source of rent and capital the source of profits and interest, is merely a distributive phenomenon and conceals the fact that labour is the only socially relevant source of output. This is the significance of the value theory and the transformation analysis to Marx." (Baumol(1), p.59.)

That is, the kernel of Marx's theory of value lies in the fact that it explains the social source of profit, and the source of profit is obscured by the social system itself, because the transformation of values into prices is necessitated by private ownership of capital in the sense that prices guarantee efficient utilization of each component of capital in all production lines. [11)]

4. Criticism of Marx proceeds further.

The fundamental Marxian theorem states the "equivalence" of the positivity of the profit rate and the rate of surplus value. Steedman and Samuelson cast a question on the validity of the theorem in this respect.

Samuelson maintained, first, that Marx's theory of value and surplus value could have been discovered in terms of orthodox economics if orthodox economics had tried, and, secondly, that the fundamental Marxian theorem and the theory of transformation can be construed, in the opposite direction to Marx, as an explanation of the rate of surplus value in terms of the profit rate: he developed a crude "parody" so as to demonstrate the fundamentality of price to value. (Samuelson (4), p.417.)

Steedman also maintained that the fundamental Marxian theorem would not constitute a positive explanation of the positivity of the profit rate, because "it runs both ways." (Steedman (4), p.58.) Moreover, he wrote:

> "Böhm-Bawerk, one of Marx's most significant neo-classical critics, did *not* seek to deny the existence of surplus labour but sought rather to show that it existed *because of* 'time preference' and the 'productivity of roundabout production'." (Steedman (4), p.58.)

In other words, variants of the fundamental Marxian theorem could be obtained if orthodox economics were to start from a different notion.

They have two critical comments here: first, equivalence explains nothing, and, secondly, even neoclassical economics can render a basis for the positivity of the profit rate, such as time-preference, or the productivity of roundabout production; hence, labour is not source of profit.

5. Now, as to which side of the fundamental Marxian theorem should explain the remainder, there will be no room for discussion. Unequivocally, the real world or the phenomenal world is the world of price, and not the world of value. One of the duties of science is to explain phenomena, but phenomena on no account explain themselves.

Accordingly, it is relevant to read the fundamental Marxian theorem in such a way that value and surplus value explain price and profit. Note that in the fundamental Marxian theorem, the equivalence of the two is stated as the synthesis of the two destinations: there exists value and surplus value behind price and profit, i.e., necessity = a descending direction, and value and surplus value are transformed into prices and profit respectively, i.e., sufficiency = an ascending direction. An interpretation of equivalence should be made carefully, but one should not reject its importance.

Whether or not labour alone can be the relevant source of profit may be beyond the scope of a mathematical discussion, so that this point will not be treated further in this volume.

Nevertheless, it must be reconfirmed that Marx's value theory based on the concept of labour is consistent in the sense that the relationships among goods, i.e., the production price system, is based on the relationships among men in production, i.e., the value system.[12)] The core of Marx's theory of value resides in the fundamental Marxian theorem.

It is also important to confirm that the fundamental Marxian theorem presents a basis for the discussion of the market. It discloses why profit is possible in the market, but gives no further clue to the functions of the market.

Orthodox economics has been concerned with explaining the functions or the behaviour of the market, whilst Marxian economics has been concerned rather with the basis of the market -- why profit is possible. Unambiguously, the two have differnt objectives -- they discuss different aspects of the capitalist economy. In this respect, Morishima is right in saying that Marx and Walras are two major disciples of Ricardo.

Finally, it is worth mentioning that the fundamental Marxian theorem discloses a superhistorical basis for the possibility of growth, on which exploitation can be based. In this sense, the theorem gives a clue to the foundation of exploitation: where there is no reproducibility, there can be no exploitation: exploitation is the process in which the reproducibility of the economy -- based on surplus labour -- is realized in the form of capital accumulation by private ownership of the means of production and the commoditisation of labour-power.

CHAPTER II

FIXED CAPITAL AND THE THEORY OF VALUE

Introduction

The framework of the Leontief economy reveals at the same time its limitations. The validity of Marx's theory of value would soon be queried, if the conditions which stipulate the Leontief economy were removed one after another.

This short chapter is devoted to introducing an economy in which the existence of fixed capital is permitted: (F.1) will be removed.[1)]

It is von Neumann that first tried to apply the analytical framework of joint-production to solving problems of fixed capital, though joint-production itself was, as in the production of meat and leather, noticed by classical economics. Namely, von Neumann regarded aged fixed capital of age s employed in a production line at the beginning of a certain period as being transformed into fixed capital of age s+1 at the end of the period: aged fixed capital is jointly produced with other types of goods. The framework of joint-production is adopted in this chapter in so far as fixed capital is concerned, but joint-production in general will still be disregarded.

The two sections discuss value, price and quantity systems with reference to fixed capital which functions with constant efficiency until used up. Value and price, and the fundamental Marxian theorem in the case of constant efficiency have been discussed by Okishio-Nakatani and Shiozawa [1]. In this chapter, the quantity system is also discussed, and the whole discussion will be reviewed in the context of the dual dualities. The purpose of doing so is that an important characteristic of value and price analysis is made clear if fixed capital is introduced.

§ 1. Value and price in a narrow plain economy.

1. An economy which admits fixed capital alone as a joint-product is called a *plain economy*, if it satisfies the following conditions: (Shiozawa [1].)

(F.5a) Fixed capital has a finite durability.

(F.5b) The efficiency of fixed capital is constant irrespective of its age.

(F.5c) No cost is required to scrap used up fixed capital.

(F.5d) No process produces aged fixed capital alone as its net product.

A plain economy restriced by the following additional condition is called a *narrow* plain economy:

(F.5e) Aged fixed capital is nontransferable.

Namely, an economy satisfying (F.5a) through (F.5e) as well as (F.2) through (F.4) is called a narrow plain economy.

Suppose that there are n types of 0-year-old good in the economy, all employable both as fixed capital and nondurable capital goods, if the difference in ages is disregarded. These n types of good are called the *basic type* of good. Let

τ_j : durability of good j as fixed capital,

$\tau = (\tau_1, .., \tau_n)$: durability vector,

and the economy has Σ types of good formally, if aged fixed capital is regarded as a different type of good, where

(1) $$\Sigma = \sum \tau_j .$$

These Σ types of good are called the *formal types* of good.

Without loss of generality, the first n types of good of all Σ kinds of good can be regarded as 0-year-old goods. A numbering of 0-year-old goods is called a *basic order*. A numbering of goods from 1 to Σ, which is called a *formal order*, is completed by arranging the groups of goods from 0-year to the maximum age, in each age group goods being ordered in the basic order.

Take the processes producing good i, and suppose that fixed capital is allocated as follows: the first process is equipped with 0-year-old fixed capital alone, and fixed capital in process s is older than that in process s-1 by one year except that which should be replaced owing to wear and tear by fixed capital of 0-year: fixed capital of process s-1 is carried over to process s. Thus, the cycle of processes, such as process 1 ---> process 2 ---> .....---> process T ---> process 1, is considered, where

(2) $$T = \text{l.c.m.}(\tau_1,\ldots,\tau_n) .$$

The set of T processes is called an industry. As each industry consists of T processes, there are nT processes in the economy, and hence a narrow plain economy is formally an economy made of nT processes producing Σ types of goods: albeit in a restricted sense, (F.2) is relaxed.

Nevertheless, a narrow plain economy can be regarded as an economy producing n types of goods of the basic types with n industries, which is called the *Leontief-basis* of the economy.

The combination of inputs of process 1 in an industry determines that of other processes in that industry, in the sense that the amounts of labour and other material inputs are the same irrespective of the ages of fixed capital and the combinations of fixed capital of other processes are derived from that of process 1. Hence, the combination of inputs of process 1 in each industry is called the *basic* one in each industry.

The combination of fixed capital in the first process of each industry is composed of only 0-year-old fixed capital, so that this combination can be expressed by an n x 1 vector, called basic fixed capital inputs. Fixed capital inputs of other processes are expressed by Σ x 1 vectors according to the formal types of good, whereas nondurable capital goods are 0-year-old goods, and hence their inputs are expressed by n x 1 vectors fundamentally.

For industry i, let

${}^{\nu}\tilde{k}^i$	$\Sigma \times 1$:	fixed capital input of process ν ,
k^i	$n \times 1$:	basic fixed capital input vector,
a^i	$n \times 1$:	nondurable capital goods input vector,
L_i	:	labour input,
$K^{*i} = ({}^1\tilde{k}^i,\ldots,{}^T\tilde{k}^i)$	$\Sigma \times T$:	fixed capital input matrix,
$A^i = (a^i,\ldots,a^i)$	$n \times T$:	nondurable capital goods input matrix,
$A^{*i} = \begin{pmatrix} A^i \\ 0 \end{pmatrix}$	$\Sigma \times T$:	enlarged nondurable capital goods input matrix,

$L^i = (L_i, \ldots, L_i)$ $\quad 1 \times T$: labour input vector,

Then, the input structure of the economy as a whole is represented by

$$\mathbb{A} = (K^{*1} + A^{*1}, \ldots, K^{*n} + A^{*n}) ,$$

and

$$\mathbb{L} = (L^1, \ldots, L^n) .$$

As for the output structure, let us distinguish the output of brandnew goods and that of aged fixed capital: for industry i, let

$^{\nu}\tilde{b}^i$ $\quad \Sigma \times 1$: aged fixed capital output of process ν,

$B^{*i} = ({}^1\tilde{b}^i, \ldots, {}^T\tilde{b}^i)$ $\quad \Sigma \times T$: aged fixed capital output matrix,

$I^{*i} = (e^i, \ldots, e^i)$, $\quad \Sigma \times T$: 0-year-old goods output matrix,

and the output matrix of the economy as a whole is expressed by

$$\mathbb{B} = (B^{*1} + I^{*1}, \ldots, B^{*n} + I^{*n}) .$$

Bearing in mind the cycles of processes, one has

(3) $$^{\nu}\tilde{b}^i = {}^{\nu+1}\tilde{k}^i - {}^{\nu+1}\tilde{k}^i_I ,$$

where $^{\nu+1}\tilde{k}^i_I$ is obtained by replacing the n+1-th through Σ-th elements of $^{\nu+1}\tilde{k}^i$ by zeros, and $^{T+1}\tilde{k}^i = 0^{\Sigma}$. Hence,

(4) $$B^{*i} = K^{*i}E^T - \begin{pmatrix} I_n & 0 \\ 0 & 0 \end{pmatrix} K^{*i}E^T ,$$

where $E^T = (e^2, e^3, \ldots, e^1)$, $T \times T$, is a permutation matrix.

2. Since the input-output relationships have been made clear, the value and price systems can be established. Let

$K = (K^1, \ldots, K^n)$ $\quad n \times n$: basic fixed capital input matrix,

$A = (a^1, \ldots, a^n)$ $\quad n \times n$: basic nondurable capital input matrix,

$L = (L^1, \ldots, L^n)$ $\quad 1 \times n$: basic labour input vector,

F $\quad n \times 1$: wage goods bundle,

w $\quad 1 \times n$: value vector of 0-year-old goods,

w^o $\quad 1 \times (\Sigma - n)$: value vector of aged fixed capital,

$\tilde{w} = (w, w^o)$ $\quad$: value vector,

p	$1 \times n$:	price vector of 0-year-old goods,
p^o	$1 \times (\Sigma - n)$:	price vector of aged fixed capital,
$\tilde{p} = (p, p^o)$	:	price vector,
π	:	profit rate,
$\omega = pF$	:	wage rate,
$\psi_i(\pi) = \dfrac{1}{\sum_o^{\tau_i - 1} (1+\pi)^s}$	:	rate of depreciation (by the annuity method),
$\psi = (\psi_1, \ldots, \psi_n)$	:	depreciation-rate vector.

Now, the value system of all formal types of goods can be expressed as

(5) $$\tilde{w}\,\mathbb{B} = \tilde{w}\,\mathbf{A} + \mathbf{L}\ ,$$

which can be reduced to

(6) $$w = w(\hat{\tau}^{-1}K + A) + L\ .$$

Likewise, its price system

(7) $$\tilde{p}\,\mathbb{B} = (1+\pi)\tilde{p}(\mathbf{A} + F\,\mathbf{L})$$

can be reduced to

(8) $$p = p\left[\pi K + \hat{\Phi}(\pi)K + (1+\pi)(A+FL)\right]\ ,$$

Namely, the value and price systems, (5) and (8), appear to be undetermined, but values and prices of 0-year-old goods are determined respectively independently of those of aged fixed capital.[2)]

Write

$$\Psi(\pi) = \pi K + \hat{\Phi}(\pi)K + (1+\pi)(A + FL)\ ,$$

and it is easy to see that Pd.C. and Pf.C. can apply to (5) and (8).

Let us assume:

(A.1) $A \geqq 0\ ,\ K \geqq 0\ ,\ \tau_i > o\ ;\ F \geq 0^n$.

(A.1) $L_i > o$.

(A.3) $\Psi(o)$ is indecomposable.

And, define the rate of surplus value as before by

(9) $$\mu = \frac{1}{wF} - 1\ .$$

Then, Okishio-Nakatani proved:

THEOREM I. (Fundamental Marxian theorem) There exist $\pi > o$ and $p \geq 0_n$ satisfying (8), if and only if $\rho(\hat{\tau}^{-1}K+A) < 1$ and $\mu > o$.

§ 2. The quantity system and replacement in kind.

1. The replacement of fixed capital in kind will be considered from the side of the quantity system, and it will be compared with the depreciation of fixed capital in the world of value and/or price.

Suppose that the economy is in the state of uniform growth. Let

x^i $\quad T \times 1$: intensity vector of industry i,

$x = \begin{pmatrix} x^1 \\ \vdots \\ x^n \end{pmatrix}$ $\quad nT \times 1$: intensity vector of the economy,

$\mathbb{F} = \begin{pmatrix} F \\ 0^{\Sigma-n} \end{pmatrix}$ $\quad \Sigma \times 1$: enlarged wage goods bundle,

q_i : output of good i,

$q = \begin{pmatrix} q_1 \\ \vdots \\ q_n \end{pmatrix}$ $\quad n \times 1$: output vector of goods of 0-year,

g : uniform growth rate,

U $\quad n \times 1$: capitalists' consumption vector,

$U^* = \begin{pmatrix} U \\ 0^{\Sigma-n} \end{pmatrix}$ $\quad \Sigma \times 1$: enlarged capitalists' consumption vector,

$\mathbb{K} = (K^{*1}, \ldots, K^{*n})$: fixed capital input matrix of the economy,

$\iota = (\iota_1, \ldots, \iota_n)$: the replacement rate vector, $(\iota_i(g) = \psi_i(g).)$

Now, the system of equations of uniform growth is expressed by

$$\text{(10)} \qquad \begin{pmatrix} q \\ 0^{\Sigma-n} \end{pmatrix} + (B^{*1}, \ldots, B^{*n})x = (1+g)(\mathbb{K} + \mathbb{A} + \mathbb{F}L)x + U^* ,$$

which can be reduced to

$$\text{(11)} \qquad q = \left(\hat{\iota}(g)K + gK + (1+g)(A + FL)\right)x + U .$$

The right hand side of (11) indicates the allocation of goods, i.e., replacement, accumulation and capitalists' consumption in the quantity system on the Leontief-basis.

2. It is easily seen that the coefficient matrix of (11) can be written as $\Psi(g)$, so that (11) is rewritten as

$$\text{(11')} \qquad q = \Psi(g)q + U .$$

The subsequent theorem soon follows.

THEOREM II.(Fundamental duality) The existence of $g > o$ and $q \geq 0^n$ fulfilling (11') is equivalent to the existence of $\pi > o$ and $p \geq 0_n$ satisfying (8).

That is, on the Leontief-basis of a narrow plain economy, strong fundamental duality holds, as in a Leontief economy: the possibility of growth and profitability are equivalent on the Leontief-basis.

The rate of profit, however, does not coincide with the rate of growth, so that the volume of depreciation will not equal to the amount of replacement in kind. Let us discuss this quantitative difference between the two in what follows.

In view of the well-known Cambridge equation, one has

$$g \leqq \pi ,$$

so that

$$\psi(\pi) \leqq \iota_i(g) \leqq \iota_i(o) = \frac{1}{\tau_i} ,$$

Hence, if the capitalist class consumes part of the profit, the amount of depreciation falls short of the amount of replacement in kind; hence, profit is greater than net investment + capitalist consumption by that amount of shortfall:

$$(12) \qquad \pi p(K+A+FL)q = gp(K+A+FL)q + pU + \left(p\hat{\iota}(g)Kq - p\hat{\iota}(\pi)Kq\right).$$

Since, from the angle of maintaining the quantity of fixed capital, the "true" volume of depreciation should be evaluated on the basis of the rate of replacement, i.e., the growth rate, and not the rate of depreciation, i.e., the profit rate, part of depreciation should come from profit in the form of overdepreciation[3] -- the ( ) part in (12).

Nevertheless, one has

$$\frac{d}{dg}\left(\frac{p\hat{\iota}(g)Kq - p\hat{\iota}(\pi)Kq}{\pi p(K+A+FL)q}\right) < o ,$$

so that this "overdepreciation" has a brake effect on capitalists' consumption.

Moreover, the maximum of the rate of depreciation is the rate of replacement, and the maximum of the rate of replacement is the rate of replacement in the world of value. If an economy in the state of simple reproduction with positive profit is contemplated, the rate of replacement is evaluated by $1/\tau_i$ for fixed capital i. This suggests that the value system is rather related to the zero-growth than to the zero-profit state of the economy.

This suggestion can be illustrated as follows.

Take an economic variable x_t representing the state of the economy, say output. Suppose that the actual locus of the economy is represented by $A_1 A_2 .. A_n$. To assume that the economy is in the state of simple reproduction is to approximate the actual dynamic locus by a set of line-segments, $\overline{A_j B_j}$s, where A_j and B_j are given by (j, x_j) and $(j-1, x_j)$ respectively.

FIGURE II-1.

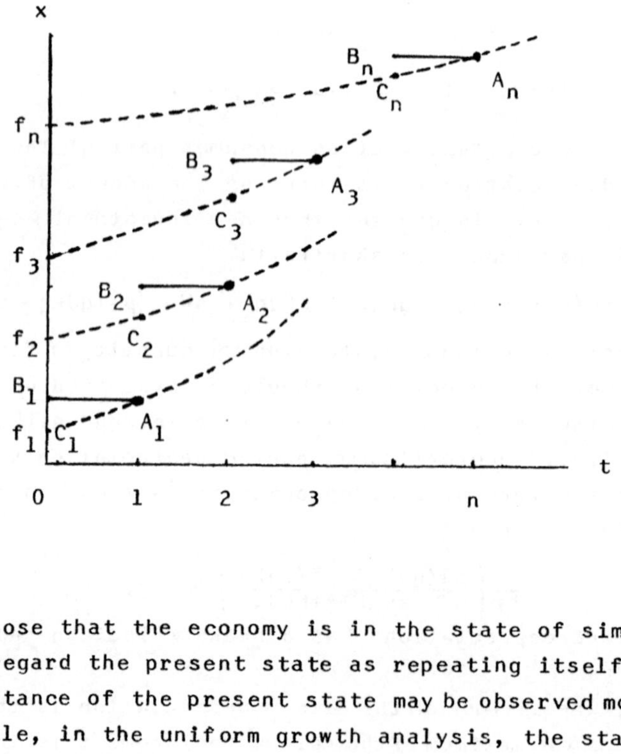

To suppose that the economy is in the state of simple reproduction is to regard the present state as repeating itself. By doing so, the substance of the present state may be observed more precisely.

Meanwhile, in the uniform growth analysis, the state of the economy is approximated by uniform growth paths. Given technical conditions and wages, the uniform growth rate g_t will be evaluated, and $f_t = (1+g_t)^{-1} x_t$. Then, the actual economic locus is approximated by the set of $\widehat{A_j C_j}$s, where C_j is given by $(j-1, (1+g_j)^{j-1} f_j)$.

3. So far, it has been shown that the value and price systems of a narrow plain economy can be reduced to their subsystems with respect to 0-year-old goods, and that uniform growth can be considered only within the Leontief-basis of the original narrow plain economy.

Moreover, it must be noted that the reduction of the quantity system of a narrow plain economy to that of the Leontief basis, i.e., (10) to (11), is slightly different from the reduction of the value and/or price systems, in the sense that formally different kinds of goods should be aggregated together in the reduction of the quantity system. Since the "true" volume of amortisation is evaluated in the quantity system, the above means that the core of the annuity method resides in the identification of aged fixed capital of the same basic type.

Nevertheless, it can be confirmed that a narrow plain economy is represented by its Leontief-basis in the sense that its productiveness, profitability and reproducibility are respectively equivalent to their counterparts of the Leontief-basis.

Observe, however, that the narrow plain economy constructed above represents a type of stationary state: if the investment of 0-year-old fixed capital is commenced simultaneously at a certain period and continued thereafter, and if fixed capital is utilized till it is worn out physically, and if there is no market for aged fixed capital, then the state of the economy will be that of a narrow plain economy.

Although, in the framework of the narrow plain economy, froc aging, i.e., fixed capital is not used but ages in a production process idly, or storage of fixed capital cannot be treated because of (F.5e), the framework of the narrow plain economy can be applied to and enrich econometric analyses, if the fixed capital coefficients are known.

4. If the efficiency of fixed capital changes as it ages, the framework of analyses should be extended further, which will be discussed in the following chapters.

CHAPTER III

JOINT-PRODUCTION AND THE THEORY OF VALUE

Introduction -- Problems.

1. It has been demonstrated that Marx's major conclusions are valid in a Leontief economy or a narrow plain economy. In such an economy, however, alternative processes, fixed capital and joint-production are not admitted to their full extent.

An economy in which alternative techniques, fixed capital and joint-production are permitted without any restriction is called a *von Neumann economy*. That is, an economy with a set of linear techniques is called the von Neumann economy, if restricted by (F.4) alone. A highly generalised discussion of value theory can be carried out in the framework of the von Neumann economy, because the von Neumann economy represents a developed, complex and modern structure of production.

The objective of this chapter is to develop the Marxian value theory in the von Neumann economy case by employing a system of equations and to investigate some implications.

2. Morishima and Steedman are the ones who pointed out the difficulties which Marx's theory of value may come up against in the von Neumann economy. (Morishima(4), Ch.14, Steedman(1).) Their discussion and counterexamples will be summarized by way of introduction.

Morishima's point is that value can take a negative magnitude. According to Morisima, Marx's value theory ought to treat the values of products as weights of the aggregation of microscopic industries into macroscopic major departments, and then values are required to be "(a) non-negative, (b) unique and (c) independent of what happens in the market."(Morishima(4), p.181.) However, it is easily seen that the requirement (a) is not satisfied in the following case.

Let an economy have two types of good and one type of labour. Goods are called good 1(nondurable capital goods), good 2(new fixed capital) and good 3(aged fixed capital). The input-output structure of the economy is expressed by the following table:

TABLE III-1.

	input matrix			output matrix		
good 1	0.7	0.9	0.2	1	1	0
good 2	0.5	0	0	0	0	1
good 3	0	0.5	0	0.5	0	0
labour	1	1	0.5	-	-	-

By solving the following value system:

$$w_1 + 0.5w_3 = 0.7w_1 + 0.5w_2 + 1 ,$$

$$w_1 = 0.9w_1 + 0.5w_3 + 1 ,$$

$$w_2 = 0.2w_1 + 0.5 ,$$

one has $w_1 = 7.5$, $w_2 = 2.0$, and $w_3 = -0.5$. That is, although the above economy is productive, the value of good 3 is negative.[1)]

Steedman went one step further and exemplified not only the possibility of negative value but also the coexistence of negative surplus value and positive profit.

Given a 2 good-2 process economy described as follows:

TABLE III-2.

	input		output		wage goods
good 1	5	0	6	3	3
good 2	0	10	1	12	5
labour	1	1	-	-	-

Since the economy is productive, there exist positive prices and a positive profit rate: from

$$(1+r)5p_1 + 1 = 6p_1 + p_2 ,$$

$$(1+r)10p_2 + 1 = 3p_1 + 12p_2 ,$$

one has $r = 20\ \%$, $p_1 = 1/3$ and $p_2 = 1$, where wages are paid ex post.

The values of goods are, however, determined as:

$$5w_1 \quad + 1 = 6w_1 + \quad w_2 \ ,$$

$$10w_2 + 1 = 3w_1 + 12w_2 \ ,$$

and, $w_1 = -1$ and $w_2 = 2$. Assume here that 5 units of process 1 and 1 unit of process 2 are operated. Then,

total labour = 6 ,

total variable capital = 7 .

Hence, it soon follows that

surplus value = - 1 ,

even if the profit rate is positive.

Thus, Steedman cast a question on the validity of the fundamental Marxian theorem: he maintained that Marx's theory of value should be rejected as something redundant.

Our following discussion will make it clear why these counter-examples are made possible.

§ 1. Productiveness, value and inferior processes.

1. Let there be n processes producing m kinds of good in a von Neumann economy. The input-output structure of the economy is expressed by

A	m x n	:	input matrix,
B	m x n	:	output matrix,
L	1 x n	:	labour vector.

Let

$D = B - A$: net production matrix,

$\tilde{D} = \begin{pmatrix} D \\ -L \end{pmatrix}$: activity matrix .

And, D defines the *production possibility space* of net products:

$$\mathbb{P}(D) = \{Dx \mid x \geqq 0^n.\}$$

As usual, let

x n x 1 : intensity vector,
y m x 1 : net product vector,

and the net product vector is defined by

(1) $$y = Dx .$$

As mentioned before, the fundamental requisite of an economy is that it is productive. The productiveness condition of a von Neumann economy will be stated as

(Pd.C) $$\exists\, x \geqq 0^n : Dx > 0^m .$$ 2)

In a productive economy, for a $y > 0^m$, (1) has a solution $x \geqq 0^n$: so that there exists a generalised inverse of D such that:

(2) $$DD^- y = y .$$

The solution of (1) can be thus expressed as

(3) $$x = D^- y .$$ 3)

The strong productiveness condition is given by

(S.Pd.C) For $\forall\, y \geqq 0^m$, $\exists\, x \geqq 0^n$: $y = Dx$.

As is easily seen, strong productiveness implies productiveness, but, as opposed to the Leontief economy case, the converse is not true in the von Neumann economy case. The production possibility space of a strongly productive economy contains the first quadrant of the goods space, $\mathbb{R}^m_+$, i.e.,

$$\mathbb{R}^m_+ \subseteqq \mathbb{P}(D) ,$$

but that of a productive economy has some points in common with $\mathbb{R}^m_+$, i.e.,

$$\mathbb{R}^m_+ \cap \mathbb{P}(D) \neq \emptyset .$$

Now, as usual, let us assume:

(B.1) $A \geqq 0$, $B \geqq 0$, $L \geq 0_n$.

PROPOSITION 1. S.Pd.C. ==> $\exists\, D^- \geq 0$.

Proof.

Put $y = e^j$, j=1,..,n, in (3), and the conclusion soon follows.

Q.E.D.

The converse is not true. In fact, there are productive eocnomies having $D^- \geqq 0$, but which are not strongly productive.

A nonnegative matrix $(I-A)^{-1}$ can be invariably considered in a Leontief economy, because S.Pd.C. is equivalent to Pd.C. therein. In a von Neumann economy, however, a generalisation of $(I-A)^{-1} \geqq 0$, i.e., $D^- \geqq 0$, can be made only in a restricted case. This is the first point to be taken note of.

2. The first definiton of value by Marx, i.e., M_1-value, can be extended as follows.

Let

w $1 \times n$: M_1-value vector,

and the value equation system can be extended to

(4) $$wB = wA + L \ .$$

A solution of this defines M_1-value.

Equation (4), however, is not invariably solvable. Therefore, let the following condition be introduced:

(V.S) $$\text{rank } D = \text{rank } \tilde{D} \ .$$

This is a necessary and sufficient condition for the solvability of (4), and is rewritten as

(5) $$LD^-D = L \ .$$

This condition means that the labour vector L and each row of the matrix D are mutually constrained: the rows of D represent how net products are allocated to the processes, and L is affected by this form of allocation.

A simple Leontief economy satisfies V.S., whilst a Leontief economy which is generalised in such a way that alternative techniques are permitted does not.[4)] Plain economies fulfil V.S.

If V.S. is satisfied, then (4) is solvable, and its solution can be written as

(6) $$w = LD^- \ .$$

Since a generalised inverse of a rectangular matrix D contains parameters, it is not unique. Hence, M_1-value expressed by (6) is not unique, even if it exists. The introduction of V.S. is the second point to be taken note of.

Now, let us consider the axiom called the impossibility of land of Cockaigne (Koopmans, p.50.):

(Im.C) $\{ x \mid \tilde{D} x \geq 0^{m+1},\ x \geqq 0^n \} = \emptyset$.

Next, the indispensability of labour in production can be represented as:

(Id.L) $x \geqq 0^n$ and $Dx \geq 0^m \Longrightarrow Lx > o$.

Then, one can show:

PROPOSITION 2. (Im.C) $\Longleftrightarrow$ (Id.C) .

Proof.

(Im.C) is equivalent to the fact that, for $\forall\ x \geqq 0^n$, $\tilde{D}x \geq 0^{m+1}$ does not hold. If one has $x \geqq 0^n$ and $Dx \geq 0^m$, then it follows that $-Lx < o$, i.e., $Lx > o$: (Id.C) holds.

The converse is trivial. Q.E.D.

In what follows, the subsequent assumption will be made:

(B.2) Labour is indispensable in production: (Id.L) holds. [5)]

Investigate next whether or not positive values exist in a von Neumann economy satisfying V.S.

PROPOSITION 3. Assume V.S. Then,

$$wy = Lx \ .$$

Proof.

From (5) and (6), one has

$$wy = LD^{-}Dx = Lx \ . \qquad \text{Q.E.D.}$$

PROPOSITION 4. Assume V.S., and M_1-value of at least one good is positive: $w \nleqq 0^m$.

Proof.

Since $Lx > o$ for $y \geq 0^m$, it follows that $w \nleqq 0_m$ in view of Proposition 3. Q.E.D.

As is seen from the above, all the values of products cannot be negative. Nevertheless, some products may have negative values, which was what Morishima and Steedman argued.

In order to disclose why negative value becomes possible, let the subsequent definition be introduced:

DEFINITION 1.(Inferior processes) Processes belonging to category J are said to be inferior to processes belonging to category I (with respect to product s), if there exist $k_t \geqq o$ such that

(7) $$\sum_{i \varepsilon I} k_i \tilde{d}^i \geq \sum_{j \varepsilon J} k_j \tilde{d}^j \ ,$$

(> for product s), where $I, J \subset \{1,\dots,n\}$, $I \cap J = \emptyset$ and $\tilde{d}^i$ is the i-th column of $\tilde{D}$.[6)]

Unambiguously, inferior processes of J produce, in comparison with processes of I, less net amount of product s with a greater amount of input. It should be observed here that the inferiority of processes does not depend on the valuations of goods.

Then, one can show:

THEOREM I. M_1-values are positive, if and only if there is no inferior process operating in the economy.

Proof.

One has only to apply Stiemke's theorem. In fact, the operation of inferior processes is equivalent to the solvability of $\tilde{D} z \geq 0^{m+1}$, which is in turn equivalent to the fact that there exists no positive solution $\tilde{w} > 0_{m+1}$: $\tilde{w}\tilde{D} = 0_n$. Namely, in such a case, there exists no $w > 0_m$, where $\tilde{w} = (w,1)$. (Cf. Lemma 13.) Q.E.D.

Having a closer look at the "only if" part of the theorem, the information on which goods have nonpositive values can be obtained.

COROLLARY. At least one of the values of the goods, in the production of which some processes are inferior, is nonpositive.

Proof.

Without loss of generality, one may divide the processes and goods into two groups: processes I are not inferior, whilst processes II are inferior to I in the production of good II. No process is inferior in the production of good I. Then, one can partition D, L and w as:

$$D = \begin{pmatrix} D_{I\,I} & D_{I\,II} \\ D_{II\,I} & D_{II\,II} \end{pmatrix}, \quad L = (L_I, L_{II}), \quad w = (w_I, w_{II}).$$

Equation (4) can be rewritten as

$$\text{(8)} \qquad \begin{aligned} w_I D_{I\,I} + w_{II} D_{II\,I} &= L_I , \\ w_I D_{I\,II} + w_{II} D_{II\,II} &= L_{II} , \end{aligned}$$

whereas, for a $z = {}^t(z_I, z_{II}) \geqq 0^n$, (7) is written as

$$\text{(9)} \qquad \begin{aligned} D_{I\,I} z_I &= D_{I\,II} z_{II} , \\ D_{II\,I} z_I &> D_{II\,II} z_{II} , \\ L_I z_I &\leqq L_{II} z_{II} . \end{aligned}$$

Postmultiply the two equations in (8) by z_I and z_{II} respectively, and subtract both sides of the results. In view of (9a) and (9c), one has

$$w_{II}(D_{II\,I}z_I - D_{II\,II}z_{II}) < o \ .$$

In the light of (9b), $w_{II} \not\geq 0_{\partial}$, where ∂ = card. J . Q.E.D.

It must be observed that one cannot say anything about w_I .

The above theorem and its corollary expound why Morishima and Steedman encountered negative values: their counterexamples contain inferior processes.[7)]

3. Productiveness plays a central role in a Leontief economy, being equivalent to the existence of positive M_1-value. Such a strong duality, however, does not hold in a von Neumann economy. Neither the solvability of the value equation nor the inferiority of processes depends on the productiveness of the economy. This is the third point to be taken note of.

A class of von Neumann economies as a straightforward extension of the Leontief economy may be formed as follows.

First, it is easy to see that a strongly productive economy is an immediate extension of the Leontief economy, if V.S. is satisfied. In a strongly productive economy, one has:

PROPOSITION 5. Assume V.S. Then, S.Pd.C. $\Longrightarrow$ $w \geqq 0_m$.

In fact, in view of Proposition 1, one gets, $w = L D^- \geqq 0_m$.

The core of this straightforward extension resides in the point that $D^- \geqq 0$. Hence, the class of von Neumann economies satisfying

(P.g.I) $\exists\ D^- \geqq 0$.

may be considered. It is easy to see that P.g.I. is weaker than S.Pd.C.

In the ensuing discussion, P.g.I. is often referred to, because the class of economies satisfying this presents an interesting angle to the argument of the value theory in the von Neumann economy case, and not because it is of importance.

§ 2. Alternative definitions of value.

The aim of this section is to introduce alternative definitions of value and investigate their equivalence.

The second definition of the value of goods by Marx, i.e., M_2-value, is defined by the amount of labour directly or indirectly necessary for the production of a unit of its net product. (Definition I-4).

As opposed to the Leontief economy case, M_2-value cannot be defined in terms of equality, because a general joint-production system cannot produce only a unit of net product of a certain kind without extra output of other kinds of product. Therefore, M_2-value should be formulated in terms of an inequality.

Let

w^* $1 \times m$: M_2-value vector,

and M_2-value is defined by

(10) $$w_i^* = \min \{ Lx^i \mid Dx^i \geqq e^i, \; x^i \geqq 0^n . \}$$

Then, one can show:

THEOREM II. There exists a unique M_2-value in a productive von Neumann economy: Pd.C. $\Longrightarrow$ $\exists \; w^* \geqq 0_m$.

Proof.

If Pd.C. holds, then the linear programming problem (10) has an optimum solution, and hence w_i^* is unique and nonnegative.

Q.E.D.

That is, M_2-value is related to the productiveness of the economy.

Compare M_1-value with M_2-value, and one has:

PROPOSITION 6. Assume Pd.C. and V.S.

(i) If M_1-value is positive, then it does not exceed M_2-value: $w \geq 0_m \Longrightarrow w^* \geqq w$.

(ii) M_1-value is equal to M_2-value, if and only if S.Pd.C. holds: $w = w^* \Longleftrightarrow$ S.Pd.C.

Proof.

(i) Premultiply (10) by $w = LD^-$ ($\geq 0_m$), and one has

$$Lx^i = LD^-y^i \geqq LD^-e^i ,$$

i.e., $w^* \geqq w$, where $y^i = Dx^i \geqq e^i$.

(ii) It is trivial that $w^* = w$ if and only if $y^i = e^i$ for $\forall$ i, which is in turn equivalent to S.Pd.C. Q.E.D.

As is seen from the above, M_1-value does not generally coindide with M_2-value in a von Neumann economy. The existence of M_2-value rests on the productiveness of the economy, but M_1-value is not related to it. On the other hand, in a Leontief economy, S.Pd.C. and Pd.C. are equivalent, and V.S. is also satisfied, so that M_1-value is equal to M_2-value. Moreover, there exists no inferior process therein owing to (F.1). This is the fourth point to be taken note of.

Now, consider:

DEFINITION 2.(Marginal value) The marginal value of a product is the amount of labour directly or indirectly necessary to increase a unit of its net product. This is also termed *M_3-value*.

Let

w^{**} $1 \times m$: marginal value vector,

and it can be formulated as

(11) $$w^{**}_i = Lx^{*i} - Lx^i,$$

where,

$$Bx^i = Ax^i + y, \quad x^i \geqq 0^n,$$

$$Bx^{*i} = Ax^{*i} + y + e^i .$$

The relationship between M_1-value and M_3-value is made clear by the following:

PROPOSITION 7. Assume $\text{rank}(B-A) = m \leq n$. Then, V.S. implies

$$w = w^{**} .$$

Proof.

$\text{rank}(B-A) = m \leq n$ implies that the subspace $\mathbb{P}(D)$ is an m-dimensional convex cone, and hence $\exists$ $y \in \mathbb{P}(D)$: for $\forall$ $i \in \{1,..,m\}$, $y+e^i \in \mathbb{P}(D)$. It follows that

$$w^{**}_i = Lx^* - Lx^i = LD^- e^i,$$

so that $w = w^{**}$. Q.E.D.

Note that w^{**} appears to rest on y, but, as shown by the above, it does not in fact do so.

The product LD^- itself exists invariably, and if the assumption of the above is satisfied, LD^- represents M_3-value. Since it does not depend on V.S., it is less restrictive than M_1-value. Nevertheless, the M_3-value of some goods can be negative.

Morishima proposed the definition of value as being shadow price.

DEFINITION 3.(Optimum value) An optimum solution of the following linear programming problem:

(12) $$\text{Max}\,\{\Lambda q \mid \Lambda B \leq \Lambda A + L\ ,\ \Lambda \geq 0_m\}$$

is called the optimum value of products with respect to q.

The dual problem of (12) is described by

(13) $$\text{Min}\,\{Lx \mid Bx \geqq Ax + q\ ,\ x \geqq 0^n\ .\}$$

The following proposition states how M_1-value and M_2-value are related to the optimum value.

PROPOSITION 8. Let Λ^o be the set of the solutions of (12).

(i) Assume Pd.C. Then, $\Lambda^o \neq \emptyset$.

(ii) Assume Pd.C., V.S. and $q \subseteq \mathbf{P}(D)$. Then, $w \geqq 0_m$ implies that M_1-value is an optimum value: $w \geqq 0_m \Longrightarrow w \in \Lambda^o$.

(iii) Assume S.Pd.C. Then, M_2-value is an optimum value: $w^{**} \in \Lambda^o$.

Proof.

(i) If Pd.C. holds, it is trivial that (13) has an optimum solution. Hence, an optimum value exists.

(ii) Since $q \subseteq \mathbf{P}(D)$, there exists $x = D^-q \geqq 0^n$, for which

$$\min Lx = \min LD^-q = \min wq$$

holds; whilst, from $\Lambda D \leqq L$ in (12), it follows that

$$\Lambda DD^-q = \Lambda q \leqq LD^-q = wq\ .$$

That is, w is an optimum solution of (12).

(iii) There exists $x^j = D^-e^j$, and for $q = \sum_j q_j e^j$, one has

$$\min Lx = \min LD^- \sum q_j e^j = \sum w^*_j q_j = \max \sum \Lambda_j q_j\ .$$

Namely, $w^*_j = \Lambda_j$, if $q = e^j$. Q.E.D.

Optimum value, defined in terms of the inequality, will be discussed in the next chapter.

In what follows, the following assumption will be made:

(B.3) The economy is productive: Pd.C. is fulfilled.

§ 3. Profitability and reproducibility -- The fundamental Marxian theorem.

1. The ultimate purpose of capitalist production is the production of profit and its appropriation. The fundamental Marxian theorem that grasps surplus value as the source of profit has been challenged by Steedman as mentioned in the introduction to this chapter.

First, let the rates of surplus value and surplus labour be formulated as before. Let, as usual,

$F \quad m \times 1$: wage goods bundle,

and make the following condition:

$$(B.1^2) \qquad F \geq 0^m .$$

The rate of surplus value can be defined as

$$(14) \qquad \mu(w) = \frac{1}{wF} - 1 ,$$

if the amount of value created by a unit of labour is normalized as unity. $\mu(\ )$ indicates that μ depends on the valuations of goods.

As is easily seen, if V.S. holds, μ can be evaluated.. M_1-value however, is not unique, so the magnitude of the rate of surplus value cannot be determined uniquely.

Now, the necessary output vector can be extended to the necessary intensity vector: let

$\bar{x} \quad n \times 1$: necessary intensity vector,

and this is defined by

$$(15) \qquad D\bar{x} = FLx .$$

Then, the rate of surplus labour can be defined by

$$(16) \qquad \eta = \frac{Lx}{L\bar{x}} - 1 .$$

Consider here a dual condition of V.S. concerning the wage goods bundle:

$$(Wg.C) \qquad F \in \mathbb{P}(D) .$$

This condition means that the economy can produce the exact amount of goods necessary for the reproduction of labour-power without any extra amount of products. In such a case, (15) can be solved with respect to $\bar{x}$: Wg.C. implies

(17) $$DD^{-}F = F \ .$$

The converse, however, is not true.

As for the two definitions of surplus, one has:

PROPOSITION 9. If V.S. and Wg.C. hold, then

(18) $$\mu(w) = \eta \ .$$

Proof.

From V.S. and Wg.C., it follows that

$$L\bar{x} = LD^{-}FLx = wFLx \ .$$

Hence, from (14) and (16), (18) holds. Q.E.D.

The set of dual conditions, V.S. and Wg.C., holds in a productive Leontief economy, because Pd.C., being equivalent to S.Pd.C. therein, ensures Wg.C. as well as V.S. Hence, the following corollary is trivial:

COROLLARY. Assume V.S. and S.Pd.C. Then, $\mu(w) = \eta$.

Observe that

$$\mu(w^*) \geqq \mu(w) \ ,$$

and that

$$\mu(w^{**}) = \mu(w) \ ,$$

in so far as the condition specified in Proposition 7 is fulfilled.

2. Let us next consider profitability in general. Let

p	$1 \times m$:	valuation vector,
Π	$1 \times n$:	processwise profit vector,

and write,

(19) $$M = A + C \ , \ C = FL \ , \ H = B - M \ .$$

The profitability condition is now expressed by

(Pf.C) $$\exists\, p \geq 0_m : pH > 0_n \ .$$

The profit vector is defined by

(20) $$\Pi = pH \ .$$

It is plausible to suppose that profit accrues if no wage is paid. Hence, the primitive profitability condition may be introduced:

(P.Pf.C) $$\exists\, p \geq 0_m : pD > 0_n \ .$$

This condition is always fulfilled in a productive Leontief economy.

Now, the following theorem can be established:

THEOREM III. (Fundamental Marxian theorem) Assume Wg.C.

(i) If an economy is profitable, then the rate of surplus labour is positive: Pf.C. $\Longrightarrow$ $\eta > o$.

(ii) Suppose V.S. holds. Profitability implies the positivity of the rate of surplus value: Pf.C. and V.S. $\Longrightarrow$ $\mu(w) > o$.[8)]

Proof.

(i) Pf.C. implies that there exists $p \geq 0_m$, such that

$$pD - pC > 0_n .$$

Postmultiply this by $D^-FLx \geq 0^n$, and one has

$$(pDD^-F - pCD^-F)Lx = pF(Lx - L\bar{x}) > o .$$

Since $p \geq 0_m$ and $F \geq 0^m$, it follows that $pF > o$. Hence, $Lx - L\bar{x} > o$, i.e., $\eta > o$.

(ii) Trivial in view of Proposition 9. Q.E.D.

COROLLARY. Assume P.Pf.C. and P.g.I. The positivity of the rate of surplus value implies profitability: $\mu(w) > o \Longrightarrow$ Pf.C.

Proof.

If $\mu > o$, there exist $p \geq 0_m$ and $\Pi > 0_n$ such that

$$p = \Pi D^-(I-Fw)^{-1}$$

in the light of P.g.I. and Lemma 7. Then, one has

$$pD - pFLD^-D = \Pi D^-D .$$

Hence, from V.S. and P.Pf.C., there exist $p \geq 0_m$ and $\Pi > 0_n$ such that $pD - pC = \Pi > 0_n$. Q.E.D.

As is made clear by the above theorem, Steedman's counterexample concerns the economy that does not fulfill Wg.C.

3. The surplus condition can be written as:

(S.C) $\quad \exists\, x \geqq 0^n$: $Hx > 0^m$.

Let

s m x 1 : surplus products vector,

and this is determined by

(21) $$s = Hx .$$

The relationship between reproducibility and the rate of surplus value is expressed by the following:

PROPOSITION 10. Assume V.S.

(i) If $w \geqq 0_m$, then S.C. implies $\mu > o$.

(ii) Suppose Wg.C. and P.g.I. $\mu > o$ implies S.C.

Proof.

(i) S.C. implies that there exists $x \geqq 0^n$ such that

$$Dx - Cx > 0^m.$$

Premultiply this by $w = LD^- \geqq 0_m$, and it follows that

$$LD^-Dx - LD^-Cx > o ,$$

so that, in view of V.S.,

$$Lx - wFLx = (1-wF)Lx > o .$$

Since $Lx > o$ from (B.2), one has $1-wF > o$, i.e., $\mu > o$.

(ii) Write tentatively $v = D^-F$. Then, $wF = Lv$, so that $(I-Fw)^{-1} \geqq 0$ is equivalent to $(I-vL)^{-1} \geqq 0$. (Cf. Lemma 7.)

If $\mu > o$, then from the assumption, there exist $x \geqq 0^n$ and $s > 0^m$ fulfilling

$$x = (I-vL)^{-1}D^-s .$$

Then, it follows that

$$Dx - DD^-FLx = DD^-s ,$$

which is reduced to

$$Dx - Cx = s ,$$

in the light of Wg.C. and Pd.C. Q.E.D.

In summary, one can state:

THEOREM IV. Assume V.S., Wg.C., P.Pf.C. and P.g.I. The positivity of the rate of surplus value, profitability and reproducibility are all equivalent.

That is, the strong fundamental duality of profitability and reproducibility, as observed in a Leontief economy and a narrow plain economy, does not hold in a von Neumann economy. It now rests on the set of dual conditions, V.S. and Wg.C., and the positive valuations of products. This is the fifth point to be taken note of.

4. Let us introduce the rate of profit. As usual, let

π : profit rate .

The equilibrium profitability condition is written as

(E.Pf.C) $\exists\ \pi > o$, $p \geq 0_m$:

(22) $$pB = (1+\pi)pM .$$

It is trivial that E.Pf.C. implies Pf.C., hence Theorem III can apply. Consider here, however, its converse.

Introduce the subsequent condition:

(P.Pf.C') $\exists\ p \geq 0_m\ ,\quad \pi^M > o\ :\ pB = (1+\pi^M)pA\ ,$

which is a modification of P.Pf.C., and make the following two assumptions:

(B.4) $1_m M > 0_n\ ,$

(B.5) P.PF.C'. holds.

Assumption (B.4) means that in each process direct and/or indirect input is required.

The fundamental Marxian theorem with respect to the equilibrium profit rate is stated as:

THEOREM V.(Fundamental Marxian theorem) Assume Wg.C.

(i) Equilibrium profitability is equivalent to the positivity of the rate of surplus labour: E.Pf.C. $\Longleftrightarrow$ $\eta > o$.

(ii) Suppose V.S.. Equilibrium profitability is equivalent to the positivity of the rate of surplus value: E.Pf.C. $\Longleftrightarrow$ $\mu(w) > o$.

Proof.

(i) In view of Wg.C., one has $\bar{x} = D^{-}FLx \geq 0^n$. Postmultiply (22) by this, and it follows that

$$pD\bar{x} = pC\bar{x} + \pi pM\bar{x}\ .$$

Namely,

$$\pi pM\bar{x} = pF(Lx - L\bar{x}) = pF\eta L\bar{x}\ .$$

If $pF = o$, $\pi > o$ is ensured by (B.5). The converse is true in the light of Theorem III.

If $pF > o$, then, owing to (B.4), $\pi > o \Longleftrightarrow \eta > o$.

(ii) Trivial in the light of Proposition 9. Q.E.D.

As shown by this theorem, the set of dual conditions, V.S. and Wg.C., is crucial in the explanation of the positivity of the profit rate by the positivity of the rate of surplus value based on M_1-value. If the two are satisfied, the fundamental Marxian theorem holds true, even if some values are not positive.

5. The determination of the production prices and the profit rate by (22) may be regarded as an extension of that in a Leontief econ-

omy, if some additional conditions are satisfied.

PROPOSITION 11. Assume V.S., Wg.C., P.g.I. and rank $H = m$ [9].
Then, $\pi > o$ and $p \geq 0_m$ are determined by the Frobenius root of $Q = MH^-$ and the eigen vector associated with it as:

$$\pi = \frac{1}{\rho(Q)}, \qquad p = \rho({}^tQ) .$$

Proof.

π and p satisfying (22) also fulfil $pH = \pi pM$, i.e.,

$$p = \pi p MH^- ,$$

in view of Lemma 11(ii).

Now, V.S. implies $R({}^tC) \subseteq R({}^tD)$, and E.Pf.C. implies $\mu > o$ owing to Theorem IV, so that it follows that

$$H^- = D^-(I-Fw)^{-1} \geqq 0 .$$

Hence, $MH^- \geqq 0$. Therefore, Frobenius' theorem can apply. Q.E.D.

§ 4. Transformation theorems.

1. The purpose of this section is to show that the transformation of M_1-value into price is possible in a certain restricted von Neumann economy.

Let us consider a transformation formula in the von Neumann economy case on the basis of Proposition 11. Consider the following sequences $\{w^t\}$ and $\{\pi^t\}$:

$$(23) \qquad w^{t+1}H = \pi^t w^t \cdot M , \qquad \pi^t = \frac{w^t \cdot Hx}{w^t \cdot Mx} ,$$

where $w^o = w$, $x \in \mathbb{R}^n_+$. [10]

Repeating (23), one has:

PROPOSITION 12. For any $x \in \mathbb{R}_+^n$ the following holds:

$$w^{t+1} Hx = w^t \cdot Hx \ , \quad (t = 0,1,2,\dots).$$

In fact, postmultiply (23a) by x, and take (23b) into account. The conclusion soon follows.

This proposition shows that the transformation formulae specified by (23) transform values into prices keeping the total profit equal to the total surplus value in each iteration step.

PROPOSITION 13. Assume that V.S., Wg.C., P.g.I. and rank $H = m$ hold, and that $Q = MH^-$ is indecomposable and stable. If $\mu > o$, then:

(i) The sequence generated by (23) is convergent, and

$$p^{**} = \lim_{t \to \infty} w^t = \theta({}^tQ) \ ,$$

$$\pi = \lim_{t \to \infty} \pi^t = \frac{1}{\rho(Q)} \ .$$

(ii) $$p^{**}Hx = wHx \ .$$

Proof.

(i) Since rank $H = m$, (23a) can be rewritten as

$$w^{t+1} = \pi^t w^t \cdot MH^- \ .$$

Now, $\mu > o$ implies that $(I-Fw)^{-1} \geqq 0$, i.e., $H^- \geqq 0$ in view of Lemma 7. Hence, $Q = MH^- \geqq 0$. Because of the indecomposability and stability of Q, the convergence of the sequences generated by (23) is proved in the same manner as in Okishio (4).[11)]

(ii) Trivial in the light of Proposition 12. Q.E.D.

The price vector p^{**} satisfies (12) by dint of Proposition 11. It represents an absolute production price in the sense that it is normalized so as to yield the equality of the total profit and the total surplus value.

2. In the case of transforming M_1-value into price, Proposition I-7 can be formally extended to:

PROPOSITION 14. If any two of the subsequent three equalities, i.e.,

$$pBx = wBx \ ,$$
$$pMx = wMx \ ,$$
$$pHx = wHx \ ,$$

hold true, then the remaining one is also true.

(The proof is trivial.)

Since $p = p^{**}$ implies the equality of the total profit and the total surplus value ($pHx = wHx$), total price $\doteq$ total value is now equivalent to total cost price = total cost value. In order to investigate this a little further, let us consider the dual aspect of (22).

Introduce the von Neumann growth path. Let

x^c $n \times 1$: von Neumann proportion,

g^c : von Neumann growth rate.

These are determined by

$$(24) \qquad Bx^c = (1+g^c)Mx^c \; .$$

The set of g^c and x^c, thus defined in terms of equality, defines, together with π and p in (22), the von Neumann equilibrium in the present restricted economy.

PROPOSITION 15. Assume V.S., Wg.C., P.g.I. and rank $H = m$. Then, $\eta > o$ implies that g^c and x^c are determined respectively by the Frobenius root of $Q^* = H^- M$ and the eigen vector associated with it as:

$$g^c = \frac{1}{\rho(Q^*)} \quad , \quad x^c = \Theta(Q^*) \; .$$

Proof.

Wg.C. implies $R(C) \subseteq R(D)$, so that $H = D(I-D^-C) = D(I-vL)$, where $v = D^-F$. If $\eta > o$, then $(I-vL)^{-1} \geqq 0$, owing to Lemma 7, and hence it follows that

$$H^- = (I-vL)^{-1}D^- \geqq 0 \; .$$

Namely, $Q^* = MH^- \geqq 0$, because of Lemma 12. Since g^c and x^c satisfying (24) also fulfill

$$x^c = g^c Q^* x^c \; ,$$

the rest of the proof is trivial in view of Lemma 2. Q.E.D.

Now, in the present case, the following can be derived:

COROLLARY. (i) $\pi = g^c$.

(ii) $$p^{**}Bx^c = wBx^c \; .$$

(iii) $$\pi = \frac{\mu}{1 + \xi(x^c)} \; .$$

(The proof is trivial.)

Thus, it is seen that in the class of economies considered here, the transformation of values into prices is possible.

§ 5. Conclusions.

1. The discussion developed in this chapter shows how the concepts which are equivalent in the Leontief economy case are different in the von Neumann economy case, and, at the same time, displays the difficulties of Marxian value theory which is based on the value equation: five related points are mentioned in our discussion.

The solvability of the value equation in a von Neumann economy is severed from the productiveness of the economy, so that V.S. itself should be assumed in the M_1-value based analysis. M_1-value is no longer equal to M_2-value in general.

It must be emphasized that the straightforward fundamental duality between profitability and reproducibility does not hold in the von Neumann economy case. In order to establish it, some contions and especially nonnegative values are seen to be necessary. This leads to the introduction of the concept of value. This is one of the most important results obtained in this chapter.

As M_1-value differs from M_2-value, so does the rate of surplus value differ from the rate of surplus labour. In order to prove the fundamental Marxian theorem on the basis of M_1-value and the rate of surplus value, the condition on wage goods, Wg.C., should be introduced together with V.S.: these two constitute a dual set of conditions. If Wg.C. is not fulfilled, Steedman's counterexample makes sense.

Note that if Wg.C. is fulfilled, the fundamental Marxian theorem can be established in terms of the rate of surplus labour, even if V.S. does not hold. This gives an important clue to the further generalisation of Marxian value theory.

2. Even if M_1-value exists, its positivity is not related to the productiveness of the economy. M_1-value is positive if and only if there is no inferior process operating in the economy.

Steedman maintained, however, that at a sufficiently high rate of profit even an inferior process can be operated.

Steedman's criticism here is made on the basis of the wage-profit curve theory. Let us note, however, that the discussion of the choice of techniques based on the wage-profit curve does not take into account the dynamic aspect of how techniques are chosen.

Since the employment of a process is commenced by investment, let us ask in which phase of the economic dynamic process, especially business cycles, investment embodying new techniques is made. A possible Marxian explanation of business cycles and the choice of techniques would go as follows: investment embodying new techniques is started in the depression phase, and not in the boom phase: in the depression phase, a huge amount of capital is scrapped and new processes embodying advanced techniques will be introduced; in the boom phase, investment will be made extensively, not necessarily accompanied by technical development. If this were to be the case, techniques employed at a very low level of the profit rate in the depression phase could never be inferior, and hence positive values of goods would be obtained.

3. Nevertheless, it is obvious that the above Marxian view is a weak explanation. What is learnt from Theorem IV is that values should be positive and they must be related to the evaluation of the rate of surplus, so that a more relevant explanation is required.

As pointed out in the above, there is room for the concept of M_2-value and the rate of surplus labour to be generalised further: the condition Wg.C. is required in the proof of the fundamental Marxian theorem based on surplus labour in this chapter simply because the necessary intensity vector is defined in terms of the equality. This generalisation will be made in the next chapter.

CHAPTER IV

MARX-VON NEUMANN'S THEORY OF VALUE

Introduction.

The theory of value based on the system of value equations comes up against a crucial difficulty in a von Neumann economy, unless the additional conditions as discussed in the preceding chapter are fulfilled. To presuppose such conditions will, needless to say, circumscribe the validity of Marx's theory of value,

If the value equation is not solvable, the rate of surplus value cannot be evaluated. There still remains the possibility, however, that the rate of surplus labour reflects the volume of surplus. How then is the rate of surplus labour defined in general terms?

Although Morishima put forward a criticism of Marx's value theory with Steedman, he went a step further to pave the way for the generalisation of Marx's value theory: he reconstructed Marx's value theory in terms of the inequality á la von Neumann, and discussed the relevance and significance of the fundamental Marxian theorem. The discussion of the fundamental Marxian theorem and related topics á la von Neumann, originally adovocated by Morishima (5) and Morishima-Catephores, is called Marx-von Neumann's theory of value in this volume.

The purpose of this chapter is to place Marx-von Neumann's theory of valuo in the development of value theory.

The same framework and the notation as employed in Chapter III will be used and similar assumptions will be made. The basic assumptions are:

(B.1) $A \geqq 0$, $B \geqq 0$, $L \geq 0_n$, $F \geq 0^m$.

(B.2) $x \geqq 0^n$ and $Dx \geq 0^m \implies Lx > o$.

(B.3) The productiveness condition holds: $\exists\, x \geqq 0^n$: $Dx \geqq 0^m$, (W,Pd.C).

Note that the set of techniques A , B and L in this chapter is that of technically possible techniques. Also note that the productiveness condition can be weakened here. The remaining assumptions and conditions will be introduced as the discussion proceeds.

§ 1. The theory of optimum value.

1. In order to evaluate the amount of surplus in general terms, let us begin with the following definiton:

DEFINITION 1.(Minimum necessary labour) The smallest amount of labour necessary for the production of the wage goods distributed to the workers is called minimum necessary labour.

Let

x^a n x 1 : actual intensity vector,

and for a given x^a, consider the subsequent linear programming problem: (LP.A)

$$(1) \qquad \operatorname{Min} \{ Lz \mid Bz \geqq Az + FLx^a,\ z \geqq 0^n \} .$$

It is easy to see that the minimum magnitude of this gives the amount of minimum necessary labour. It is also seen that the problem represents the maximisation of the productivity of labour. In what follows, let a minimiser be called:

z^o n x 1 : necessary intensity vector.

Since minimum necessary labour represents how much the actually employed workers exert their labour so as to produce the wage goods they receive, it is natural to state:

DEFINITION 2.(Surplus labour) Surplus labour is the actual expenditure subtracted by minimum necessary labour:

$$\text{surplus labour} = Lx^a - Lz^o.$$

This is a natural extension of the definition of surplus labour previously made. Then, the rate of surplus labour can be defined by

$$(2) \qquad \eta = \frac{Lx^a}{Lz^o} - 1 .$$

This is formally the same as the traditional definition.

PROPOSITION 1. The rate of surplus labour is uniquely determined.

Proof.

(LP.A) is feasible in view of (B.1), and $Lz > o$ from (B.2). Namely, the objective function is bounded from below. Hence (LP.A) has an optimum solution, and $Lz^o = \min Lz$ is unique. (Cf. Lemmas 15-17.)

Q.E.D.

Note that the proportion of z^o does not depend on x^a.

2. Consider the dual problem of (LP.A). It is stated by: (LP.B)

$$(3) \qquad \mathrm{Max}\ \{\ \Lambda F L x^a \mid \Lambda B \leqq \Lambda A + L\ ,\ \ \Lambda \geqq 0_m.\}$$

As mentioned by Definition III-3, an optimum solution of (3) defines the optimum value with respect to FLx^a.

DEFINITION 3. (M_4-value) An optimum value with respect to FLx^a is called M_4-value, or simply optimum value.[1)]

The optimum value is the shadow price of products with respect to the minimisation of labour necessary for their production. Let

$\Lambda^o \quad 1 \times m : \quad M_4$-value vector,

and, as mentioned by Proposition III-8, a nonnegative M_4-value exists in a productive von Neumann economy. Note that the proportion of Λ^o does not depend on x^a.

In view of the duality theorem of linear programming, one has

$$(4) \qquad Lz^o = \Lambda^o F L x^a .$$

The maximum value of (3), i.e., $\Lambda^o F L x^a$, represents the volume of wages in terms of M_4-value, and hence is regarded as paid labour. Thus, the rate of unpaid labour may be defined by

$$(5) \qquad \mu' = \frac{Lx^a - \Lambda^o F L x^a}{\Lambda^o F L x^a} .$$

Next, net products are represented by

$$y^a = (B - A)x^a ,$$

so that surplus value in terms of M_4-value is given by

$$\text{surplus value} = \Lambda^o (B-A)x^a - \Lambda^o F L x^a .$$

Therefore, the rate of surplus value can be defined by

$$(6) \qquad \mu = \frac{\Lambda^o (B-A)x^a - \Lambda^o F L x^a}{\Lambda^o F L x^a} = \mu(\Lambda^o) .$$

The relationship among these three rates of surplus is stated by the following proposition:

PROPOSITION 2. $\quad \eta = \mu' \geqq \mu$.

Proof.

From (4), $\eta = \mu'$ is trivial; whereas, from (3), one has

$$\Lambda^o (B - A)x^a \leqq Lx^a ,$$

and hence,

$$\Lambda^o (B-A)x^a - \Lambda^o F L x^a \leqq Lx^a - Lz^o ,$$

by dint of (4). Thus, $\eta \geqq \mu$. Q.E.D.

Accordingly, it is seen that the rate of surplus value, which is not uniquely determined, is an incomplete measure of exploitation.

§ 2. The fundamental Marxian theorem, generalised.

1. As opposed to the Leontief economy case in which the quantitative as well as qualitative aspect of equilibrium is made clear by Frobenius' theorem, only a little has been known about equilibrium in the von Neumann economy case. The theory of von Neumann equilibrium concerns chiefly the qualitative aspect of equilibrium.

Given the technical matrices and the wage goods bundle, the von Neumann equilibrium can be defined by the solutions of the subsequent problems:

(7) $$\text{Min} \{ \pi^w \mid p^w B \leqq (1+\pi^w) p^w M \text{ , } p^w \geqq 0_m \} \text{,}$$

(8) $$\text{Max} \{ g^c \mid B x^c \geqq (1+g^c) M x^c \text{ , } x^c \geqq 0^n \} \text{ .}$$

Let, as usual,

π^w		:	warranted rate of profit,
p^w	$1 \times m$	:	von Neumann price vector,
g^c		:	von Neumann growth rate,
x^c	$n \times 1$	:	von Neumann proportion,

and the von Neumann equilibrium is described by the quadruplet, (π^w, p^w, g^c, x^c).

Now, let the subsequent assumptions be made:

(B.4) $$B 1^n > 0^m, \quad 1_m M > 0_n \text{ .}$$

The first assumption here means that each type of good is produced by at least one process. (As for the second, see p.59.)

The following proposition is well-known:

PROPOSITION 3.(i) There exists a von Neumann equilibirum, with

$$\pi^w \leqq g^c \text{ .}$$

(ii) $\pi \geqq \pi^w$, if π is the profit rate satisfying

$$p B^a = (1+\pi) p M^a, \quad p \geq 0_m \text{ ,}$$

where B^a and M^a are respectively output and augmented input matrices of the engaging processes.

(As for the proof, refer to Klein, pp.358-67.)

Let us note that the theory of von Neumann equilibrium concerns mainly the qualitative aspects of equilibrium, in the sense that it discusses the existence of equilibrium and establishes the inequality concerning the von Neumann growth rate and the warranted profit rate.

Nevertheless, von Neumann equilibrium does not exclude the case in which the economy is contracting. Since von Neumann equilibrium concerns the possibility of growth and profitability, such a case in which the von Neumann growth rate, for instance, is nonpositive is economically meaningless. Then, one has to ask under which conditions von Neumann equilibrium makes sense -- $g^c > o$ and/or $\pi^w > o$. It was Morishima that discussed the relationship between von Neumann equilibrium and the rate of surplus labour on the basis of the above problem. He thus shed light on the most important problem of modern growth theory.

Let P.Pf.C'. of Chapter III(p.59) be extended as:

(B.5) $\min \{ \pi^M \mid p^M B \leqq (1+\pi^M) p^M A ,\ p^M \geqq 0_m . \} > o$.

This means that if wages are not paid, the warranted rate of profit can be positive.

Then, Morishima demonstrated the following propositions:

PROPOSITION 4. $\eta > o$ implies $\pi^w > o$.

In fact, from (1), (2) and (7), it follows that

$$\eta p^w FLz^o \leqq \pi^w pMz^o,$$

and the conclusion is soon obtained.

PROPOSITION 5. $g^c > o$ implies $\mu' > o$.

In fact, premultiply (8) by Λ^o , and postmultiply (3) by x^c. It soon follows that

$$g^c \Lambda^o M x^c \leqq \mu' \Lambda^o FLx^c .$$

Hence, the conclusion follows.

THEOREM I. (Fundamental Marxian theorem, generalised) $\pi^w > o$, $g^c > o$ and $\eta > o$ are all equivalent.

(As for the detail of the proof of these three propositions, see Morishima(6), pp.619-21, or Morishima-Catephores, pp.51-3.)

2. Some additional discussion will be made here on an extension of Morishima-Seton's equality.

The organic composition of capital in terms of M_4-value is expressed as

(9) $$\xi(\Lambda^o, x^a) = \frac{\Lambda^o A x^a}{\Lambda^o FLx^a} .$$

Although the magnitude of the denominator is given by the maximum value of (LP.B), and hence is unique, that of the numerator is not unique. Hence, note that $\xi(\Lambda^o, x^a)$ itself cannot be unique.

Define the maximum equilibrium growth rate as

(10) $$g^M(x^a) = \max\{g \mid Bx^a \geqq (1+g)Mx^a.\}$$

Then, one can show:

THEOREM II. (Fundamental Marxian inequalities)[3)]

(i) $$g^M \leqq \frac{\mu}{\xi(\Lambda^o, x^a) + 1} .$$

(ii) $$\frac{\mu^*}{\xi^*(x^c) + 1} \leqq \pi^w \lesseqgtr g^c \leqq \frac{\mu}{\xi(\Lambda^o(x^c), x^c) + 1} ,$$

where $\xi^*(x^c) = \xi(p^w, x^c)$ and $\mu^* = \mu(p^w)$.

Proof.

(i) Premultiply (10) by $\Lambda^o(x^a)$, and, in view of (6) and (9), the inequality soon follows.

(ii) The third inequality can be proved by applying (i) to the $x^a = x^c$ case.

The first inequality can be derived in the same manner as in (i): postmultiply (7) by x^c, and rearrange the result.

Needless to say, the second comes from Proposition 3. Q.E.D.

The above (ii) gives an extension of Morishima-Seton's equality. The inequalities shown here hold with equality in the Leontief economy case.

3. How is the von Neumann equilibrium influenced by changes in the rate of surplus value?

Let the wage goods bundle F be rewritten again as

(11) $$F = cf ,$$

where

f	$m \times 1$:	standard wage goods vector,
c	:	the number of units of the standard wage goods bundle.

The rate of surplus labour can be rewritten as

(2') $$\eta = \frac{Lx^a}{\Lambda^o cfLx^a} - 1 .$$

It is easy to see that M_4-value, Λ^o, does not depend on c, and that if x^a is not influenced by c, $c\Lambda^o fLx^a$ is an increasing function of c. Hence, η is a continuous function of c, and

(12) $$\frac{d\eta}{dc} > o .$$

Now, take two different magnitudes η_1 and η_2 correponding to different c_1 and c_1, and write $M_i = A + c_i fL$, g_i^c, x_i^c and π_i^w, where $i = 1$ and 2, corresponding to these two. Then, one has:

PROPOSITION 6. $\eta_1 > \eta_2$ implies $g_1^c \geqq g_2^c$ and $\pi_1^w \geqq \pi_2^w$.

Proof.

From (12), $\eta_1 > \eta_2$ implies $M_1 \leq M_2$. Then, one has

$$Bx_2^c \geqq (1+g_2^c)M_2x_2^c \geq (1+g_2^c)M_1x_2^c .$$

Now, by the definition of g_1^c, one obtains $g_1^c \geqq g_2^c$. Likewise,

$$\pi_1^w \geqq \pi_2^w .$$ Q.E.D.

This proposition means that the interval (π^w, g^c) tends to shift upward if η is increased. The Marxian interpretation of this is that decreases in real wages are based on harder exploitation in the capitalist economy.

§ 3. Concluding remarks.

1. It has been shown so far that the fundamental Marxian theorem can be extended to the von Neumann economy case, and that the concept of optimum value is significant for the fundamental Marxian inequalities.

What was advocated by Morishima as the most relevant extension, however, was not the optimum value as discussed above, but "true" value. (Morishima-Catephores, p.37.)

DEFINITION 4. (True value) The minimum necessary labour for the production of a composite commodity Y is called its true value:

(14) $$\lambda_Y^o = \min\{ Lz \mid Bz \geqq Az + Y , \ z \geqq 0^n . \}$$

Needless to say, the true value of good i is given by $\lambda_{e^i}^o$.

Therefore, it is easily seen that the true value of good i is its M_2-value.

A remarkable property of the true value is that it is not additive: the following inequality holds,

$$\lambda^o_Y \leqq (\lambda^o_{e^1}, \ldots, \lambda^o_{e^m})Y .$$

Various critical comments have been made with respect to the nonlinearity of optimum value and true value. It must be noted, however, that the linearity of the valuation of goods is on no account necessary in so far as the fundamental Marxian theorem is concerned.[4)]

It must be observed, moreover, that the true value is no longer related to Marx-von Neumann's theory of value: the propositions in §§1-2 are not dependent on the concept of true value. The true value satisfies the three conditions of value stipulated by Morishima, but it has not yet been shown whether or not the true value is effective as a weight of aggregation.

An important role is played by the concepts of minimum necessary labour and optimum value. The concept of minimum necessary labour alone suffices to show the fundamental Marxian theorem, but the notion of M_4-value is indispensable in establishing the growth constraint and the fundamental inequalities.

Hence, the true value as introduced by Morishima may not be the "true" extension of M_2-value. M_2-value should be generalised in such a way that value is the shadow price of the composite commodity representing wage goods.[5)]

2. The theory of optimum value comprises the theory of value developed in the Leontief or narrow plain economy case.

The discussion made in the following context of "M_2-value ---> the rate of surplus labour ---> the fundamental Marxian theorem and the fundamental inequalities" is completely reconstructed in Marx-von Neumann's theory of value. Moreover, it is seen that the generalised fundamental Marxian theorem now manifests the fundamental duality once discarded in Chapter III: the positivity of the rate of surplus labour is necessary and sufficient for the fundamental duality to hold.

It is also easy to see that if $\pi^w > o$ and $p^w \geq 0_m$, then $\Lambda^o \geq 0_m$. This can be construed as the value basis of price, albeit in a weak sense.

3. It is worth mentioning that the rate of surplus labour is measured in a set of techniques that minimises the expenditure of labour, and that this set is usually different from the set which determines the ongoing profit rate. This can be illustrated by the following figure.

FIGURE IV-1.

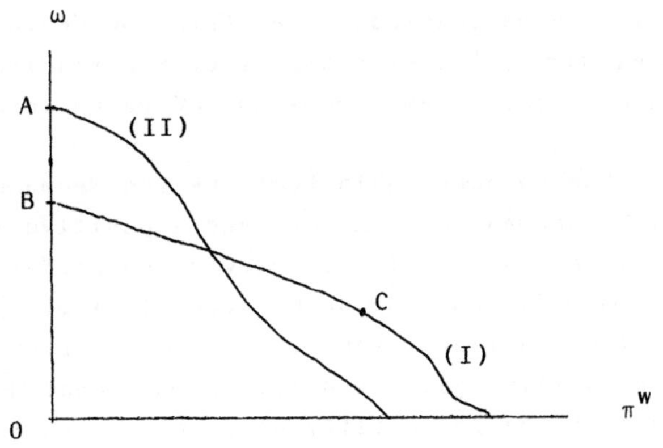

Write $I \subset \{1,..,n\}$, and $I(x) = \{ i \in \{1,...,n\} \mid x_i > o \}$, and $I(x)$ is the index set of the engaging processes for a given level of operation x.

Suppose that a particular x^a is given, which fixes the set of the engaging processes $I(x^a)$, called technique(I), and that the von Neumann equilibrium corresponding to a given F (=cf) is at point C.

The minimisation of labour in (LP.A), however, fixes a set of processes $I(z^o)$, called technique(II). Therefore, the rate of surplus labour is measured at point A on the basis of technique(II), and not at point B corresponding to technique (I).

Nevertheless, it is not necessary to evaluate the rate of surplus labour at point B, because the fundamental Marxian theorem states that the warranted profit rate at point C is positive if and only if the rate of surplus labour at point A is positive. Moreover, since $I(z^o)$ does not depend on x^a, point A represents the state in which the minimisation of labour in the given technically possible processes is attained. This is a remarkable feature of the fundamental Marxian theorem established here, because the set of the technically possible processes does not depend on the market.

This fact is important when the durability of fixed capital with changing efficiency is considered. The economic durability of fixed capital depends on the profit rate if its efficiency is changing, and is supposed to be shorter than its physical durability. The above remark means, however, that in establishing the fundamental Marxian theorem it is not necessary to take into account the dependence of the economic durability of fixed capital on the profit rate.

4. Thus, it can be concluded that Marx-von Neumann's theory of value succeeds the qualitative aspect of the traditional value theory, and as such, is an extension of value theory.

5. Let us observe here again that the von Neumann equilibrium with a positive von Neumann growth rate and a positive warranted profit rate concerns the possibility of growth and profitability of an economy, and that it is not the actual equilibrium. Nevertheless, such an economically meaningful von Neumann equilibrium represents a growing economy with positive profit in the sense that its existence is equivalent to the possibility of growth -- whether or not balanced -- and the profitability of the economy.

It is important to note that the theory of von Neumann equilibrium becomes a truly economically meaningful theory if based on the fundamental Marxian theorem.

CHAPTER V

REDUCTION OF HETEROGENEOUS LABOUR

Introduction -- Problems.

1. Heterogeneous capital has already come up for a wide discussion in economic literature, but various types of heterogeneous labour having unequal wage rates have been rarely discussed, although they are also observable in an economy. The reason for this seems to be, at the outset, that one of the aims of economic analysis is to make clear the distributional relations between capital and labour. As for capital goods, there is no distributional difficulty, even if they are heterogeneous, because an equal rate of profit is applied to them.

In Marx's economics, however, which reveals that the expenditure of labour forms value, and that it is divided into necessary and surplus labour, heterogeneous labour raises an important problem. The amounts of different types of labour expended are embodied in unequal amounts of labour even if they are expended in an equal duration of time, and thus create unequal magnitudes of value, and hence enter into the total amount of labour with unequal weights. In Marx's economics, therefore, the problem of heterogeneous labour concerns production theory.

Marx naturally took notice of heterogeneous labour. Namely, he grasped the heterogeneity of labour as the difference between skilled and unskilled labour, and pointed out, albeit very briefly, how skilled labour is reduced to unskilled labour. This is called the reduction problem in Marx's economics. Nevertheless, this was not developed in *Capital*, and the incompleteness of Marx's treatment was challenged by Böhm-Bawerk in later years. It was Hilferding that made a defence of Marx and showed the correct destination in explaining the reduction of skilled labour to unskilled labour. (Cf. Sweezy (2).)

2. An overview of the reduction of skilled to unskilled labour will be stated here according to Marx and Hilferding.

When Marx referred to the notion of commodity value, he was forced to mention the difference between skilled and unskilled labour. That is, he wrote:

"It(mere human labour) is the expenditure of simple labour-power, i. e., of the labour-power which, on an average, apart from any special development , exists in the organism of every ordinary individual. Simple average labour, it is true, varies in character in different countries and at different times, but in a particular society, it is given. Skilled labour counts only as simple labour intensified, or rather, as multiplied simple labour, a given quantity of skilled being considered equal to a greater quantity of simple labour. Experience shows that this reduction is constantly being made. A commodity may be the product of the most skilled labour, but its value, by equating it to the product of simple unskilled labour, represents a definite quantity of the latter labour alone. The different proportions in which different sorts of labour are reduced to unskilled labour as their standard, are established by a social process that goes on behind the backs of the producers, and, consequently, appear to be fixed by custom."(I.p.44)

Marx, however, presupposed:

"For simplicity's sake we shall henceforth account every kind of labour to be unskilled, simple labour; by this we do no more than save ourselves the trouble of making the reduction." (I, p.44.)

As cited above, Marx pointed out the qualitative equality and quantitative difference of skilled labour and unskilled labour, and the social character of the reduction process, but no detailed exposition was made on the matter. Then Böhm-Bawerk, criticising Marx, cast a question to the effect that one should know the amount of value created by them in order to know the reduction ratios of skilled to unskilled labour, but in turn the value of a commodity depends on the reduction ratios of skilled labour: Marx's exposition falls into tautology.

In defence of Marx, Hilferding discussed the social character of the reduction process, albeit without an analytical framework, and suggested the possibility of reducing skilled to unskilled labour in Marx's sense:

"The value-creating quality is not per se inherent in any labour. Solely in conjunction with a definite mode of social organization of the process of production does labour create value. Hence, we cannot attain to the concept of value-creating labour merely by contemplating isolated labour in its concreteness. Skilled labour, therefore, if I am to regard it as value-creating, must not be contemplated in isolation, but as part of social labour." (Sweezy (2), pp.140-41.)

Then, Hilferding proceeded:

"The question consequently arises, what is skilled labour from the social standpoint? Only when we can answer this can we expect to attain to a position from which we shall be able to recognize the principles according to which the aforesaid social reduction can be effected. Manifestly these principles can be none other than those which are contained in the law of value."(*ibid*,p.141.)

A difficulty one encounters here, however, is that one cannot apply the law of value immediately to labour itself. Nevertheless,

"We must not deduce the higher value which skilled labour creates from the higher wage of skilled labour power, for this would be to deduce the value of the product from the 'value of labour'." (*ibid.*,p.141.)

"To deduce the value of the product of labour from the wage of labour conflicts grossly with the Marxist theory. ... neither directly nor indirectly does the wage of a skilled labour power give me any information regarding the value which this labour power newly creates."(*ibid.*, pp.142-3.)

Now, how should one explain the reduction of skilled to unskilled labour in harmony with the law of value?

"Average unskilled labour is the expenditure of unskilled labour power, but qualified or skilled labour is the expenditure of qualified labour power. For the production of this skilled labour power, however, a number of unskilled labours were requisite. These are stored up in the person of the qualified labourer, and not until he begins to work are these formative labours made fluid *on behalf of society*. The labour of the technical educator thus transmits, not only *value* (which manifests itself in the form of the higher wage), but in addition its own *value-creating power*. The formative labours are therefore *latent as far as society is concerned*, and do not manifest themselves until the skilled labour power begins to work. Its expenditure consequently signifies the expenditure of all the different unskilled labours which are simultaneously condensed therein...... Thus in (a) single act of the expenditure of skilled labour a sum of unskilled labours is expended, and in this way there is created a sum of value and

surplus value corresponding to the total value which would have been created by the expenditure of all the unskilled labours which were requisite to produce the skilled labour power and its function, the skilled labour. From the standpoint of society, therefore, and economically regarded, skilled labour appears as a multiple of unskilled labour, however diverse skilled and unskilled labour may appear from some other outlook, physiogical, technical, or aesthetic."(*ibid.*, pp.144-5.)
"The more unskilled labour that skilled labour embodies, the more does the latter create higher value..."(*ibid.*, pp.145-6.)
"Thus the Marxist theory of value enables us to recognize the principles in accordance with which the social process of reducing skilled labour to unskilled labour is effected. It therefore renders the magnitude of value *theoretically measurable.*" (*ibid.*, p.146.)

In short, one type of labour is skilled labour from the social viewpoint, and a greater creativity of skilled labour is fully explained by the law of value: it is not explained by the high wages the skilled labour-power receives, but by the transmission of value-creating force from the educators to the educands in the formative process. This is the outline of Marx-Hilferding's reduction problem.

3. In order to furnish an analytical framework for reducing skilled labour to unskilled labour, let us introduce the theoretical concept, skills.

Man has, in general, the capacity to exert simple, unskilled labour. Through education, moreover, he can acquire specific capabilities which enable him to perform complex work: these are called *skills*. They are specialised types of good.

By introducing the concept of skills, the reproduction process of labour-power is conceptually divided into two parts: the production of skills and the consumption of skills, the latter, precisely speaking, being the true process in which skilled labour-power is produced.

Skills have both values and use-values: their value is the value of skilled labour-power, and their use-value is the function to enable workers to perform skilled labour. Since skills are acquired by workers, and can exist only if embodied in a worker's body, they constitute the core of skilled labour-power; skills can be identified with skilled labour-power, and their use-value with skilled labour.

An industry in which skills are produced is called an education sector. Let us note in advance the specificity of the education sectors.

Each production line is the synthesis of the labour process and the value-creating and/or augmenting process. One must look at the education sectors as such. As a value-creating process, the value of skills is produced, whilst, as a labour process, the use-value of skills, i.e., skilled labour, is "created." This, however, is not a precise expression. What takes place therein is the transference of value-creating force from the educators to the educands. Living labour is not embodied as dead labour in the education sectors, whereas it is embodied as value in the ordinary sectors.

The specificity of the education sectors will be made clearer if the following three types of metamorphosis of labour are distinguished. That is, (i) embodiment, i.e., from living to dead labour, (ii) transference, i.e., from dead to dead labour, and (iii) formation, i.e., from living to living labour. These metamorphoses constitute the cycle of labour. In this cycle of labour, the embodiment of labour is a core. In order to close the cycle of labour, however, its inverse, from dead to living labour is required, but the inverse of embodiment must not take place in the same dimension as embodiment: when dead labour constitutes the value of labour-power, its use-value becomes living labour, and acquires the potentiality to create value. Thus, the cycle of labour becomes closed and autonomously expandable. It should be noted that labour-power is specific in the sense that it is the critical point in the cycle of labour. An ordinary industry is the synthesis of (i) and (ii), whereas an education sector is that of (ii) and (iii). This consideration is the basis for solving the reduction problem.

Another point to be noted here is that the workers in the education sectors need to perform self-efforts in order to acquire qualified capabilities.

In the education sectors a given combination of capital goods and various types of formative labour is utilized. The amounts of capital goods and labour required to produce a unit of skill in the education sectors define the educational coefficients. They are defined in the same way as ordinary production coefficients are defined.

It is worth mentioning that in the present discussion workers do not possess any means of production to produce skills or skilled labour-power, because, according to Marx, workers possess no means of production, but they utilize the use-value of all the inputs into the education sectors -- for instance they rent a house, and other durable consumption goods.

Hence, it should be observed furthermore that a good called skills can be regarded as a composite commodity of both material and incorporeal inputs into the education sectors. Skills may be said to represent the comprehensive function of those inputs. That a worker consumes a unit of skill means that he utilizes this comprehensive function and reproduces his labour-power.

For the sake of convenience, the education sector for unskilled labour will also be contemplated. Thus, a complete closed economy containing the reproduction of labour-power will be expressed by an analytical framework.

4. The distinction between skilled and unskilled labour based on the formative process of skilled labour-power is socially most important for the classification of labour into variegated categories.

Another classification of various types of labour, however, is also possible. Heterogeneous labour in general, characterised only by unequal wage rates, includes such a peculiar type of labour as one based on individual talent or never linked to its formative process.

Nevertheless, according to the stance that the wage goods vector corresponding to unequal wage rates represents the requisites for the reproduction of qualified labour-power, the reduction of heterogeneous labour in general will be explained by the use of the same framework as applied to the reduction of skilled labour to unskilled labour.

The aim of this chapter is to discuss the reduction of heterogeneous labour centering around skilled labour.

In §1, Marx-Hilferding's exposition of the reduction process is investigated in the Leontief economy case. Once Okishio(2)(3) and later Rowthorn(1)(2) tackled the problem, but in our following discussion a crucial modification will be made to their system of equations to determine values and reduction ratios. After the theory of value and surplus value is dealt with in §1, the fundamental Marxian theorem and related topics are discussed in §2. Then, §3 will be devoted to a generalisation of the discussion from the Leontief to the von Neumann economy, and from the reduction of skilled labour (to unskilled labour) to that of heterogeneous labour in general. The final section, §4, introduces the discussion made from different angles by other economists on this subject, and some concluding notes will be made.

§ 1. Reduction of skilled labour to unskilled labour in a Leontief economy -- The theory of value and surplus value.

1. An economy with education sectors producing skills is called a *closed Leontief economy*, if it satisfies (F.1) through (F.3). That is, with regard to the education sectors, each sector produces a single type of skill, and there is no alternative educational process.

Suppose that n types of ordinary goods are produced, and that s types of labour are employed in the economy. Each type of labour is called labour j, $j = 1,2,..,s$, and unskilled labour is denoted by labour 1.[1)]

An industry supplying skill j is called the education sector j, and the function of a unit of skilled labour-power j is a unit of skilled labour j. A worker who performs skilled labour j is called a worker j. Hence, the number of the workers of the same type exactly mirrors the amounts of various types of labour.

The processes are divided into two departments: department I, abbreviated as dept.I, produces ordinary goods, whilst department II, abbreviated as dept.II, produces skills. As for dept.I, let

A_I $n \times n$: input matrix,

L_I $s \times n$: labour matrix,

and, as for dept. II, let

E^s	$n \times (s-1)$	: input matrix for production of skills,
T^{*s}	$(s-1) \times (s-1)$	: skilled labour matrix for production of skills,
t^*	$1 \times (s-1)$	: unskilled labour vector for skills,
$E = (0, E^s)$		: input matrix
$T^* = \begin{pmatrix} o & t^* \\ 0 & T^{*s} \end{pmatrix}$		: formative labour matrix,
n_{1j}		: the length of (exclusive) education periods for worker j,
n_{2j}		: the length of working periods of worker j,
$n_j = n_{1j} + n_{2j}$		: the average life-span of worker j.

The above information is assumed to be given.

Now, one can define:

DEFINITION 1. (Reduction ratio) A ratio of value created by skilled labour to that by unskilled labour is called the reduction ratio of skilled labour to unskilled labour.

Without loss of generality, the magnitude of value created by a unit of unskilled labour can be normalised as unity.

As for variables, let us denote:

w	$1 \times n$	: value vector of ordinary goods,
v^s	$1 \times (s-1)$	: value vector of skilled labour-power,
v_1		: value of unskilled labour-power,
$v = (v_1, v^s)$		: value vector of labour-power,
γ^s	$1 \times (s-1)$	: reduction ratios of skilled labour,
γ	$1 \times s$	: reduction ratio vector,

2. Let us construct a system of equations to determine the values of goods and labour-power, and the reduction ratios of various types of labour.

The values of goods are determined by the amounts of value transferred from the means of production added to value which is newly created by various types of labour.

(1) $$w = wA_I + L_I .$$

The reduction ratios of skilled labour are evaluated, as stated by Definition I, by the quantities of value which skilled labour can create, i.e., potentialities. Since potentialities reside in living labour itself, they must be distinguished from value (dead labour) itself.

Another closer look at the formative process should be made in advance. The value-creating force of labour exerted by the educators in the formative process is transmitted to the educands entirely: the value-creating force is retained by the educands in the form of living labour. On the other hand, goods invested in the formative process also transfer their values to the products of the process, because they are used up in production. Their value, however, is already embodied, as dead labour. The dimension of dead labour should be clearly distinguished from that of living labour. Moreover, according to the law of value, the value of goods, or dead labour, cannot be immediately transformed into value-creating force, or living labour. Thus, the value of capital goods in the education sectors cannot be added to formative labour of the educators, and hence cannot enter into the reduction ratios of skilled labour. Consequently, the reduction ratios are determined by the formative labour of the educators and the self-efforts of the educands.

Now, since the total amount of skilled labour which worker j performs during his working periods, n_{2j}, is equal to his own self-efforts over his life added to the amount of formative labour which he absorbs in his education periods, one can establish:

$$\gamma_j n_{2j} = \gamma (T^*)^j n_{1j} + n_j ,$$

namely,

$$\gamma_j = \gamma (T^*)^j (n_{1j}/n_{2j}) + (n_j/n_{2j}) .$$

Let us write:

$n = (n_{11}/n_{21}, \ldots, n_{1s}/n_{2s})$: education/working period ratio,

$T = T^*\hat{n} = \begin{pmatrix} 0 & t \\ 0 & T^s \end{pmatrix}$: augmented formative labour matrix,

$\tau = 1_s + n$ $1 \times s$: self-efforts vector,

where t and T^s are counterparts of t^* and T^{*s} respectively.

T and τ being known here, the reduction ratios are determined by

(2) $$\gamma = \gamma T + \tau \,.$$ 2) 3)

It must be observed that γL_I in (1) differs from γT in (2). The former indicates the magnitudes of value, because L_I has the dimension of labour per unit of goods, whilst the latter represents the value-creating force, for T expresses quantities of labour per unit of value-creating force: γ plays the role of an operator, which yields the quantity of value embodied in dept.I, and the level of the value-creating force transmitted in dept.II.

The problem remains: where does the value of capital goods in dept.II go? If the definition of the value of labour-power mentioned in Chapter I is recalled, it is immediately seen that it enters into the value of skills. That is, the value of skilled labour-power consists of the cost of education, which includes capital goods and skilled and unskilled labour-power in the formative process, and the value of consumption goods. As value-creating force is transmitted from the educators to the educands, so is the value of skilled labour-power through the same process.

Let us write:

F^j $n \times 1$: wage goods bundle per unit of labour j,

$F_I=(F^1,\dots,F^s)$: wage goods matrix,

$J = E + F_I$: augmented input matrix of dept.II.

The value of labour-power is now determined by

(3) $$v = wJ + vT \,.$$

Thus, the system of equations, (1) through to (3), determining the values of goods and labour-power, and the reduction ratios of skilled labour is constructed.

3. The next task is to make clear conditions under which the values of goods and labour-power and the reduction ratios determined by (1)-(3) are nonnegative, by generalising the discussion made in Chapter I.

Dept.I and II concern the production of value, irrespective of material or incorporeal, so that equations (1) and (3) can be united into one as

$$(w,v) = (w,v)\begin{pmatrix} A_I & J \\ 0 & T \end{pmatrix} + (L_I,0) \quad (4)$$

In what follows, let us call the set of dept.I and II, i.e., the sphere of value production, the *closed (Leontief) system*. Let us write:

$A = \begin{pmatrix} A_I & J \\ 0 & T \end{pmatrix}$: closed input matrix,

$L = (L_I, 0)$: closed labour matrix.

Matrices A and L above are straightforward extensions of the input matrix and the labour vector introduced in the simple Leontief economy: each row of the two represents the input structure of the process in either dept.I or dept.II.

It must be reconfirmed that, from the standpoint of formality, no labour is expended in dept.II. Namely, value-creating force is transmitted, but the labour of the educators does not create value nor is it crystallized as value immediately therein. Since the labour-power of the educators merely transfers its value to its products, i.e., skills, it must be treated as a component of constant capital.

On the other hand, equation (2) is independent: it represents the process which is not related to value production immediately and thus is concealed behind the backs of the producers.

The productiveness condition can be applied to the sphere of value production, for the input structure of value production is now revealed. Let

x_I $n \times 1$: output vector of dept.I,

x_{II} $s \times 1$: output vector of dept.II,

$x = \begin{pmatrix} x_I \\ x_{II} \end{pmatrix}$: output vector,

y_I $n \times 1$: net product vector of dept.I,

y_{II} $s \times 1$: net product vector of dept.II,

$y = \begin{pmatrix} y_I \\ y_{II} \end{pmatrix}$: net product vector,

And, one can write

(5) $$y = x - Ax \ .$$

In order to make clear the relationship between the productiveness condition concerning A and the nonnegativeness of the values and reduction ratios, let us make the following assumptions as usual:

(A.1[1]) $A_I \geqq 0$, $E^s \geqq 0$, $T^s \geqq 0$, $L_I \geqq 0$, $F^j \geq 0^n$ (for $\forall j$) .

(A.1[2]) $\tau^s > 1_{s-1}$.

(A.2) $1_s L > 0_n$.

(A.3) A_I and T^s are indecomposable.

Assumption (A.2) means that any process in dept.I requires labour input. This is a straightforward extension of the counterpart in the simple Leontief economy.

Now, a series of propositions will be verified:

PROPOSITION 1. A is productive, if and only if both A_I and T^s are productive: $\rho(A) < 1 \iff \rho(A_I) < 1$ and $\rho(T^s) < 1$.

Proof.

The productiveness of the closed system is expressed by

(6) $$(I - A)^{-1} \geqq 0 \ ,$$

namely,

$$\begin{pmatrix} I-A_I & -J \\ 0 & I-T \end{pmatrix}^{-1} = \begin{pmatrix} (I - A_I)^{-1} & (I - A_I)^{-1}J(I - T)^{-1} \\ 0 & (I - T)^{-1} \end{pmatrix} \geqq 0 \ .$$

Hence, (6) is equivalent to $(I - A_I)^{-1} \geqq 0$ and $(I - T)^{-1} \geqq 0$. Furthermore, the latter is equivalent to $(I - T^s)^{-1} \geqq 0$, and hence $\rho(T^s) < 1$ in view of (A.3). This completes the proof. Q.E.D.

In other words, the productiveness of the closed system is reduced to the productiveness of its two subsystems.

PROPOSITION 2. The productiveness of the closed system is equivalent to the existence of positive values and reduction ratios: (6) $\iff$ $\exists\ w > 0_n$, $\gamma > 0_s$.

Proof.

In view of Proposition 1, one has

$$\gamma = \tau(I - T)^{-1}$$

from (2), and

$$w = \gamma L_I(I-A_I)^{-1} > 0_n$$

from (1). Conversely, if $\gamma > 0_s$ in (2), then it follows that

$$(I-T)^{-1} \geqq 0 ,$$

because $\tau > 0_s$, and, if $w > 0_n$ and $w > wA_I$, then one has

$$(I-A_I)^{-1} \geqq 0 . \qquad \text{Q.E.D.}$$

Likewise, one can prove:

PROPOSITION 3. The productiveness of the closed system is equivalent to the existence of positive values of goods and labour power: (6) $\Longleftrightarrow \exists\, w > 0_n,\ v > 0_s$.

Consequently, if the closed system is productive, the system of equations (1), (2) and (3), or (2) and (4), can be uniquely solved, yielding:

(7) $$\gamma = \tau(I-T)^{-1},$$

(8) $$w = \tau(I-T)^{-1}L_I(I-A)^{-1} ,$$

(9) $$v = \tau(I-T)^{-1}L_I(I-A_I)^{-1}J(I-T)^{-1}.$$

(7) means that a greater value-creating force is formed behind the sphere of production through education and/or training. (9) indicates that the value of labour-power is reduced to the value of goods which are directly or indirectly required for its reproduction. Namely, (9) can be rewritten as

$$wJ(I-T)^{-1} = w(J + JT + JT^2 + \cdots) ,$$

and the first term in the bracket on the right hand side of this represents the quantity of goods directly required, and the remainder the quantity indirectly necessary.

From (4) and (5), one can easily prove:

PROPOSITION 4.

(10) $$wy_I + vy_{II} = \gamma L_I x_I .$$

The meaning of this proposition is that the volume of net products, crystallized as value, is equal to the amount of value created by labour expended in dept.I.

PROPOSITION 5. If the closed system is productive, then

(i) $$\gamma^s > 1_{s-1} .$$

(ii) $F^j \geq F^1$ implies that $v^s \geq v_1 1_{s-1}$, $(j \neq 1)$.

Proof.

(i) In the light of (A.2), it soon follows that

$$\gamma = \tau(I-T)^{-1} > \tau ,$$

which implies $\gamma^s > 1_{s-1}$.

(ii) It is easy to see that

$$v = wJ(I-T)^{-1} \geq v_1 1_s ,$$

if $F^j \geq F^1$. Q.E.D.

That is, the reduction ratios of skilled labour are greater than the level of value-creating force of unskilled labour, so that the value of skilled labour-power is normally greater than that of unskilled labour-power. It does not follow, however, that skilled labour with a greater reduction ratio is concomitant with a greater value of skilled labour-power: $\gamma_j > \gamma_i$ does not necessarily imply $v_j > v_i$.

4. Let us annex the transmittance of value-creating force, i.e., the labour process of the education sectors -- which may be called the third sphere of the economy -- to the sphere of value production. Then, equations (1) - (3) will be integrated into one system.

The closed system with the third sphere is called the *hyper-closed system*. The hyper-closed system includes all the three types of metamorphosis of labour. Let

$$\tilde{A} = \begin{pmatrix} A & 0 \\ L & T \end{pmatrix} \quad : \text{ hyper-closed input matrix,}$$

$$\tilde{\tau} = (0,0,\tau) \quad : \text{ hyper-closed labour vector.}$$

The hyper-closed (Leontief) system is described by $\tilde{A}$ and $\tilde{\tau}$. Therein one can write

$$(11) \qquad (w,v,\gamma) = (w,v,\gamma)\tilde{A} + \tilde{\tau} .$$

Since the productiveness condition can be applied to $\tilde{A}$ as before, one can establish the following:

PROPOSITION 6. The productiveness of the closed system is equivalent to that of the hyper-closed system.

Proof.

Since one has

$$(I-\tilde{A})^{-1} = \begin{pmatrix} (I-A)^{-1} & 0 \\ (I-T)^{-1}L(I-A)^{-1} & (I-T)^{-1} \end{pmatrix} ,$$

$(I-\tilde{A})^{-1} \geq 0$ is equivalent to $(I-A)^{-1} \geq 0$ in the light of Proposition 1. Q.E.D.

According to this proposition, Propositions 2 and 3 are madé up into one:

COROLLARLY. The productiveness of the hyper-closed system is equivalent to the existence of positive values of goods, labour-power and reduction ratios.

Here, let the subsequent assumption be made:

(A.4) The closed system is productive.

In the next place, consider the quantity system: let

x_{III} s x 1 : output vector of the third sphere,

$\tilde{x} = \begin{pmatrix} x \\ x_{III} \end{pmatrix}$: hyper-output vector,

y_{III} s x 1 : net product vector of the third sphere,

$\tilde{y} = \begin{pmatrix} y \\ y_{III} \end{pmatrix}$: hyper-net product vector.

What takes place in the third sphere is the transference of value-creating force, and this transference occurs simultaneously with the production of skills. The output vector of the third sphere indicates the level of value-creating force transmitted therein in terms of skilled labour. If wages are paid in advance, skills acquired by the workers employed additionally in the next period are also produced in this period.

Let us evaluate the number of workers employed in the closed system. It will be termed the *total population.* On the other hand, the number of workers employed in dept.I is called simply the quantity of *employment*: let

N^* s x 1: population vector.

Since x_{III} contains the level of value-creating force of the additional workers in the next period, it does not mirror the population of this period. Consider the simple reproduction case, and one gets the population of this period. That is, from

$$N^* = L_I x_I + T x_{III}, \qquad x_{III} = N^* ,$$

one has

(12) $$N^* = (I - T)^{-1}L_I x_I \ .$$

This shows that the total population is equal to the amount of employment directly or indirectly required in dept.I.

Now, one can establish:

THEOREM I. $$\gamma L_I x_I = \tau N^* \ .$$

Proof.

$$N^* = \tau(I - T)^{-1}L_I x_I = \gamma L_I x_I \ . \qquad \text{Q.E.D.}$$

This theorem indicates that the expenditure of various types of labour in dept.I is an accumulation of self-efforts made by the whole population.[4] One cannot overexaggerate the importance of this theorem in Marxian economics.

Let us next formulate the labour matrix and the wage goods matrix in the closed and the hyper-closed system.

Since a unit of skill j suffices for the reproduction of a unit of skilled labour-power j, as assumed previously, the formal wage goods bundle takes a specific form.

$F = \begin{pmatrix} 0 \\ I \end{pmatrix}$ n+s x s : formal wage goods matrix,

$\tilde{F} = \begin{pmatrix} F \\ 0 \end{pmatrix}$ n+2s x s: formal hyper-wage goods matrix,

$\tilde{L} = (L,0)$: hyper-labour matrix.[5]

5. Let us tackle the theory of surplus value. Three types of surplus rate will be discussed.

For labour j, let

μ_j : rate of surplus value,

μ'_j : rate of unpaid labour,

η_j : rate of surplus labour.

Since the value created by skilled labour is determined by its reduction ratio, and the value of skilled labour-power is already evaluated, one has the formula:

(13) $$\mu_j = \frac{\gamma_j}{v_j} - 1 \ .$$

The rate of unpaid labour can be defined as follows. Since part of the value-creating force of skilled labour comes from the educators, self-efforts made by the educands alone represent their net contribution; therefore,

(14) $$\text{unpaid labour} = \tau_j - wJ^j ,$$

and hence,

(15) $$\mu_j' = \frac{\tau_j}{wJ^j} - 1 .$$

The quantity of surplus labour is evaluated as follows: let

$N = L_I x_I$: employment vector ,

$\bar{x}$ n x 1: necessary output ,

$\bar{N}$ s x 1: necessary employment vector.

As argued in Chapter I , the necessary output is evaluated by

(16) $$\bar{x} = A\bar{x} + FLx .$$

Hence,

(17) $$\bar{N} = L\bar{x} = L(I-A_I)^{-1}FLx ,$$

which yields

(18) $$\text{surplus labour} = N - \bar{N} .$$

Hence, one can define

(19) $$\eta_j = \frac{N_j}{\bar{N}_j} - 1 .$$

It is easily seen from the above that the magnitude of the rate of surplus varies from one type of labour to another. Moreover, different definitions of the rate of surplus yield unequal magnitudes with respect to any type of labour.

Let us next investigate the relationship among the various rates of surplus.

Surplus value created by each type of labour is expressed by

(20) $$\gamma - v = (\tau - wJ)(I-T)^{-1} = (\tau - wJ) + (\tau - wJ)T + (\tau - wJ)T^2 + \cdots .$$

This indicates that surplus value is the unpaid labour accumulated in the formative process. From this result, one obtains:

PROPOSITION 7. If for $\forall j \quad \mu_j > o$, then for $\forall j \quad \mu'_j > o$.
Proof.

From the definition of μ_j and μ'_j, it is easily seen that for $\forall j \ \mu_j > o$ is equivalent to $\gamma - v \geq 0_s$, and that for $\forall j \ \mu'_j > o$ is equivalent to $\tau - wJ > 0_s$. In the light of (A.4), one has $(I-T)^{-1} \geqq 0$, so that from (18) it follows that $\tau - wJ > 0_s$ implies $\gamma - v > 0_s$. This completes the proof. Q.E.D.

It must be observed that the rate of unpaid labour influences the rate of surplus value.

Consider the aggregated volumes of surplus value, unpaid labour and surplus labour.

Since no labour is expended formally in dept.II, surplus value is created solely in dept.I. Thus, the following equality holds:

(21) $$\text{surplus value} = (\gamma - v)L_I x_I \ .$$

The total amount of unpaid labour is evaluated by the total self-efforts subtracted by the amount of input in the formative processes and consumption goods:

(22) $$\text{unpaid labour} = (\tau - wJ)N^* \ .$$

The total volume of surplus labour is given by

(23) $$\text{surplus labour} = \gamma(N - \bar{N}) \ .$$

These three volumes of surplus are equal:

THEOREM II. Surplus value = unpaid labour = surplus labour.
Proof.

From (16) and (17), it follows that

$$\begin{aligned} \gamma(N-\bar{N}) &= \gamma L_I x_I - wJ(I-T)^{-1} L_I x_I \\ &= (\gamma - v)L_I x_I \ , \end{aligned}$$

namely, surplus value = surplus labour; whilst

$$\begin{aligned} (\tau - wJ)N^* &= \left(\tau(I-T)^{-1} - wJ(I-T)^{-1}\right)L_I x_I \\ &= (\gamma - v)L_I x_I \ , \end{aligned}$$

i.e., unpaid labour = surplus value. Q.E.D.

That is, the amount of surplus takes the same magnitude in the dimension of value created, the expenditure of unskilled labour and the expenditure of various types of labour to create value.

Let us next evaluate the rates of socially aggregated surplus. Define

(24) $$\mu = \frac{\gamma L_I x_I}{v L_I x_I} - 1$$: social rate of surplus value,

(25) $$\mu' = \frac{\tau N^*}{wJN^*} - 1$$: social rate of unpaid labour,

(26) $$\eta = \frac{\gamma N}{\gamma \bar{N}} - 1$$: social rate of surplus labour.

Then, these three are also equal:

THEOREM III. $\mu = \mu' = \eta$.

Proof.

Let us first show that $\gamma L_I x_I = \tau N^* = \gamma N$. In fact, from the definition of N , it soon follows that $\gamma L_I x_I = \gamma N$; whilst, in view of Theorem I, one has $\tau N^* = \gamma L_I x_I$. Then, owing to Theorem II, one gets

(27) $$v L_I x_I = wJN^* = \gamma \bar{N} .$$

Therefore, $\mu = \mu' = \eta$. Q.E.D.

Note that the equality (27) in the above expresses:

variable capital = paid labour = necessary labour.

A corollary of the above may be obtained: let

$\mu^m = \min_j \mu_j$: minimum rate of surplus value,

$\mu'^m = \min_j \mu'_j$: minimum rate of unpaid labour,

$\eta^m = \min_j \eta_j$: minimum rate of surplus labour,

and,

$\mu^M = \max_j \mu_j$: maximum rate of surplus value,

$\mu'^M = \max_j \mu'_j$: maximum rate of unpaid labour,

$\eta^M = \max_j \eta_j$: maximum rate of surplus labour.

PROPOSITION 8. (i) $\mu^m > 0$ implies $\mu'^M, \eta^M, \mu > 0$.

(ii) $\mu'^m > 0$ implies $\mu^M, \eta^M, \mu' > 0$.

(iii) $\eta^m > 0$ implies $\mu^M, \mu'^M, \eta > 0$.

In fact, since μ , μ' and η are all weighted averages of μ_js, μ'_js and η_js, the proof is trivial in view of Theorem III .

6. So far, an analytical framework for Marx-Hilferding's exposition of the reduction problem has been discussed.

It can be reconfirmed that the gist lies in the creativeness of labour. Man has the capacity to exert simple, unskilled labour, but through education and training, self-efforts performed by workers are accumulated, thus forming various types of skilled labour. Self-efforts manifest themselves when the workers in dept.I perform labour of one type or another and create value. Surplus value created only in dept.I is the result of the self-efforts made by all the workers, including those in dept.II.

Observe that the equality of surplus value and surplus labour does not explicitly rest on self-efforts, which confirms the latency of reduction.

§ 2. The fundamental Marxian theorem.

1. In the system of commodity production, in which all kinds of good are produced and exchanged as commodities, skills are also subject to the law of commodity production. In the capitalist mode of production skills are also evaluated at their production prices.

Let us establish the production price system with respect to the closed Leontief system. Let

p_I $1 \times n$: price vector of ordinary goods,

p_{II} $1 \times s$: price vector of skills,

$p = (p_I, p_{II})$: price vector,

π : profit rate,

and the production price system can be described by

(28) $$p = (1+\pi)pM ,$$

where

(29) $$M = A + FL \ ,$$

Or, in detail,

$$(p_I, p_{II}) = (1+\pi)(p_I, p_{II})\begin{pmatrix} A_I & J \\ L_I & T \end{pmatrix} .$$

That is, p_{II} is the transformed form of the value of labour-power, and hence represents the wage rates of various types of labour.

The dual system of (28) is described as follows: let

x_I^c n x 1 : von Neumann proportion of dept. I,

x_{II}^c s x 1 : von Neumann proportion of dept. II,

$x^c = \begin{pmatrix} x_I^c \\ x_{II}^c \end{pmatrix}$: von Neumann proportion,

g^c : von Neumann growth rate.

Then, the von Neumann proportion and the von Neumann growth rate are determined by

(30) $$x^c = (1+g^c)Mx^c \ .$$

Note that the profitability condition and the surplus condition discussed in Chapter I can be applied to the matrix M .

Now, how can (28) and (30) be generalised to the hyper-closed system? Let

p_{III} 1 x s : price vector of labour,

x_{III}^c s x 1 : von Neumann proportion of the third sphere,

$\tilde{p} = (p, p_{III})$: hyper-price vector,

$\tilde{x}^c = \begin{pmatrix} x^c \\ x_{III}^c \end{pmatrix}$: hyper-von Neumann proportion,

$\tilde{g}^c$: hyper-von Neumann growth rate,

$\tilde{\pi}$: hyper-profit rate.

Then, equations (28) and (30) can be extended respectively to

(31) $$\tilde{p} = (1+\tilde{\pi})\tilde{p}\tilde{M} \ ,$$

and

(32) $$\tilde{x}^c = (1+\tilde{g}^c)\tilde{M}\tilde{x}^c \ ,$$

where

(33) $$\tilde{M} = \tilde{A} + \tilde{F}\tilde{L} \, .$$

It is easy to see that the enlarged value systems (4) and (11) are transformed into (28) and (31) respectively by Marx=Okishio's transformation formulae. By comparing (28) and (31), one can see what takes place in the transformation of values into prices.

First, let us show:

PROPOSITION 9.(i) $(p, 0_s)$ and π satisfy (31) if p and π satisfy (28).

(ii) If x^c and g^c satisfy (30), then $\begin{pmatrix} x^c \\ x^c_{II} \end{pmatrix}$ and g^c fulfill (32). Conversely, if $\tilde{x}^c$ and $\tilde{g}^c$ satisfy (32), then $\tilde{x}^c_{II} = \tilde{x}^c_{III}$ and $\begin{pmatrix} \tilde{x}^c_I \\ \tilde{x}^c_{II} \end{pmatrix}$, and g^c satisfy (30).

(These are derived from simple mathematical manipulation.)

The converse of the conclusion (i) must here be considered carefully. The converse of (i) is trivial, because $p_{III} = 0_s$ in (31) is the trivial solution of a subsystem of (31), i.e.,

$$p_{III} = (1+\tilde{\pi})p_{III}T \; .$$

How can this fact $p_{III} = 0_s$ in (i) be construed?

In (4) and (11), it is seen that labour-power is different from living labour. However, in the production price system, it is not obvious whether wages are paid for labour or labour-power: labour-power and labour overlap each other. The fact that $p_{III} = 0_s$ here can be construed as one of Marx's conclusions that labour has no price, although labour-power has its price, i.e., wages. Thus, comparing the closed and hyper-closed systems, one can see that in commodity production the contribution of labour to production is concealed behind labour-power, and hence the price of labour-power appears as that of labour.

The converse of (ii) is also trivial. Namely, that $x^c_{II} = x^c_{III}$ is economically plausible, because a unit of skilled labour is supposed to be based on a unit of skilled labour-power.

2. If attention is focused on M , it is easy to see that the fundamental duality holds in the closed system: the profitability of the closed system is equivalent to its reproducibility. Then, what can be said about the relationships between the positivity of the profit rate and the individual rate of surplus?

At the outset, one must recall (A.4): the closed system is productive. This guarantees that although A itself is decomposable, positive profit is possible if wages are not paid. In the form relevant to the following discussion, one can write

(34) $\exists\, p^M \geq 0_{n+s}\,,\ \pi^M > o\ :\ p^M = (1+\pi^M)p^M A\,.$

In the next stage, let us consider a degree of complexity in the classification of labour so as to make our discussion more generalised.

Namely, it should be noted that there are some types of labour which are not employed in dept.I. They are exclusively exerted in dept.II. A type of labour is said to be of the *first kind*, or *productive*, if it is employed in dept.I, and of the *second kind*, or *unproductive*, if it is solely employed in dept.II. This consideration is plausible, because in reality some types of labour, such as pure teaching work, are not employable in dept.I. As for the labour of the second kind, the elements of the row of L coressponding to it are all zeros.

Thus, it is confirmed that one of the implications of the above is that in general $Lx \geq 0^s$, instead of $Lx > 0^s$. Let

N_I k x 1 : employment vector of the first kind,

where $k \leqq s$ is the number of types of labour of the first kind.

Without loss of generality, one can write, for instance,

$$N = \begin{bmatrix} N_I \\ 0^{s-k} \end{bmatrix}.$$

(Needless to say, whether or not unskilled labour is of the first kind is not important.)

Now, let us demonstrate a series of propositions:

PROPOSITION 10. The positivity of the minimum rate of surplus labour implies the positivity of the profit rate: for $^{\forall} x > 0^n$, $\eta^m > o \Longrightarrow \pi > o$.

Proof.

The necessary output is determined by (16):

$$\bar{x} = A\bar{x} + FLx \ .$$

Rewriting the right-hand side, one has

$$(35) \qquad \bar{x} \geqq A\bar{x} + (1+\eta^m)FL\bar{x} \ .$$

Premultiply this by p satisfying (28), and

$$p\bar{x} \geqq pA\bar{x} + (1+\eta^m)pFL\bar{x} \ ,$$

whilst, from (28), one has

$$p\bar{x} = (1+\pi)pM\bar{x} \ .$$

Hence,

$$\pi pM\bar{x} \geqq \eta^m pFL\bar{x} \ .$$

(α) If $pF = 0_s$, then there exists a $\pi > o$ owing to (A,4), i.e., (34).

(β) If $PF \geq 0_s$ and $PFL\bar{x} = o$, then

$$p\bar{x} \geqq (1+\pi)pA\bar{x} \ .,$$

whereas, from $PF \geq 0_s$ and $N = Lx \geq 0^s$, it follows that

$$p\bar{x} = pA\bar{x} + pFLx \geqq pA\bar{x} \ .$$

Hence,

$$pA\bar{x} \leqq (1+\pi)pA\bar{x} \ .$$

Let us show that if $pFLx = o$ here, the present case will be reduced to the case (α). Let us denote the set of indices of productive labour by

$$<N> = \{k \,|\, (L\cdot 1^n)_k > o\} \ .$$

Since $<N> \neq \emptyset$ from (A.2), if $pFLx = o$, then for $i \in <N>$,

$$(p_{II})_i = o \ ,$$

Whereas as for labour j, where $j \in \{1,..,s\}$, $\notin <N>$, $(FL\cdot 1^n)_j = o$ holds.

Therefore, $pFLx = o$ implies $pFL = 0_s$, i.e., the case (α).

If $pFLx > o$, then $p\bar{x} \doteq pA\bar{x} + pFLx > pA\bar{x}$, i.e,, $\pi > o$.

(γ) If $pFL\bar{x} > o$, the conclusion soon follows. Q.E.D.

The converse of this proposition is not true in general. In order for the converse to hold true, the output, i.e., the variable of the quantity system, should satisfy a certain condition. Morishima-Seton's equality will give a clue to that.

First, note that the organic composition of capital in the closed system is given by

$$(36) \qquad \xi(w,x) = \frac{(w,v)FLx}{(w,v)Ax} .$$

THEOREM IV. (Morishima-Seton's equality)

$$(37) \qquad g^c = \frac{\mu(x^c)}{\xi^c(x^c)+1} ,$$

where $\xi^c(x^c) = \xi((w,v),x^c)$, and $\mu(x^c)$ stands for the social rate of surplus value aggregated by x^c.

Proof.

Premultiplying (31) by (w.v), one has

$$g^c = \frac{(w,v)x^c - (w,v)Mx^c}{(w.v)Mx^c} .$$

Bearing in mind (36), one obtains (37). Q.E.D.

COROLLARY. $g^c > o$ implies $\eta(x^c) > o$.

As shown by the above theorem and its corollary, if the von Neumann proportion is employed as weights of aggregation, the von Neumann growth rate is determined by the organic composition of capital and the social rate of surplus value evaluated on the basis of the von Neumann proportion. The positivity of the von Neumann growth rate, at the same time, implies the positivity of social rate of surplus value. Hence, if x in the vicinity of x^c is considered, the same proposition will be expected to hold.

Let us introduce here again:

$$G = \{x \mid x > Mx,\ x \geqq 0^{n+s}\}$$

which is called the growth region.

Also define, as before, the greatest equilibrium growth rate by

$$(38) \qquad g^M = \max\{g \mid x \geqq (1+g)Mx\}.$$

PROPOSITION 11. $g^c > o$ is equivalent to $G \neq \emptyset$.

Proof.

Necessity is trivial. Sufficiency is derived from Frobenius' theorem. Q.E.D.

PROPOSITION 12. $\eta^m(x) > o$ implies $\bar{x}(x) \in G$, where $\eta^m(\ )$ and $\bar{x}(\ )$ represent that they are dependent on aggregators.

Proof.

In (35), if $\eta^m > o$, then it is trivial that $\bar{x} \in G$. Q.E.D.

PROPOSITION 13. (Growth constraint)

$$(39) \qquad g^M \leqq \frac{\mu(x)}{1 + \xi(x)} \quad .$$

Proof.

Premultiply (38) by (w,v), and one soon gets (39). Q.E.D.

It is worth mentioning that Theorem IV and Proposition 13 are formally the same as Theorem I-V and Proposition I-9 respectively. This again confirms the fact that with respect to the production of value the education sectors are not different from the industries producing ordinary goods.

PROPOSITON 14. $g^c > o$ implies $\mu(x) > o$ for $x \in G$.

Proof.

$g^c > o$ implies $G \neq \emptyset$, and there exists an $x \in G$. For an $x \in G$, $g^M(x) > o$, and hence $\mu(x) > o$. Q.E.D.

PROPOSITION 15. $x \in G$ implies $\eta^m(x) > o$.

Proof.

$x \in G$ implies that $x > Ax + FLx$, and hence

$$x > \bar{x} = (I-A)^{-1}FLx \; .$$

Namely, $Lx > L\bar{x}$, and hence $\eta^m(x) > o$. Q.E.D.

In summary, one obtains:

THEOREM V. (Fundamental Marxian theorem, generalised) $\pi > o$, $g^c > o$ and $\mu(x) > o$ are equivalent for $^\forall x \in G$, and $x > 0^n$.

(In fact, $\pi = g^c$ by dint of Proposition I-8.)

3. Once heterogeneous labour is taken into account, the fundamental Marxian theorem suffers from the constraint "for $^\forall x \in G$ and $x > 0^n$". Nevertheless, this constraint is not so restrictive as might be imagined.

If the economy lies in the growth region, surplus products are actually produced. Outside the region, some sectors are contracting, and eventually negative production will occur therein. Hence, sooner or later, the economy should return to the growth region. This state of the economy can be persistent, if surplus products are produced, and hence surplus labour is performed as regards all the types of labour.

Therefore, Marxian value theory is valid for the expalanation of the possibility of long run equilibrium growth and profitability associated with it in this respect.

§ 3. A von Neumann economy with heterogeneous labour.

1. Consider the von Neumann economy in which heterogeneous labour is permitted. Such an economy is called a *closed von Neumann economy*.

In order to facilitate a clearer mathematical discussion, the von Neumann economy discussed in Chapter IV will be extended, in a straightforward manner, to include heterogeneous labour. Let

$A \quad q \times n \quad :$ input matrix,

$B \quad q \times n \quad :$ output matrix,

$L \quad s \times n \quad :$ labour matrix,

$F = (F^1,..,F^s):$ wage goods matrix .

These are assumed to be given as technical data. Furthermore, let

$x^a \quad n \times 1 \quad :$ actual intensity vector,

$N^a = Lx^a \quad :$ actual employment vector.

These are treated as parameters.

As usual, let us make the following assumptions:

(B.1) $A \geqq 0 \,,\; B \geqq 0 \,,\; L \geqq 0 \,,\; F^j \geq 0^q,\; N^a > 0^s.$

(B.2) $x \geq 0^n$ and $Bx \geq Ax \implies Lx > o$.

(B.3) $\exists\, x \geq 0^n$: $Bx \geqq Ax$ (weak productiveness).

2. Consider the subsequent linear programming problem as (LP.I):

$$\text{(40)} \qquad \text{Min} \left\{ k \,\middle|\, \begin{array}{l} Bz \geqq Az + FN^a, \\ kN^a \geqq Lz \;,\; z \geqq 0^n,\; k \geqq o \,. \end{array} \right\}$$

The first inequality constraint is easily seen to be an extension of the inequality defining necessary labour in the homogeneous labour case. What, then, does the second inequality signify?

Since it can be written as

$$k = \max_i \frac{(Lz)_i}{(N^a)_i} \;,$$

the magnitude of k represents how much of the actual employment $(N^a)_i$ should be allocated at most for the production of wage goods, because $(Lz)_i/(N^a)_i$ represents the ratio of necessary labour to the total labour expended with respect to labour i. Therefore, the necessary intensities and the least necessary labour will be determined by (LP.I).

From Proposition IV-1, for a productive von Neumann economy, in which labour is indispensable, there exists an optimum solution of (LP.I), denoted as z^o. Hence, min $k = k^o$ can be uniquely determined. These two define:

z^o : necessary intensity vector,

k^o : maximum necessary labour ratio.

Note that these two quantities depend on x^a.

According to the meaning of k, $N^a - Lz^o$ can be regarded as the surplus labour vector. Hence, the *rate of surplus labour* for labour j may be defined by

(41) $$\eta_j = \frac{(N^a)_j}{(Lz^o)_j} - 1 .$$

Since z^o is not unique, η_j cannot be determined uniquely. Moreover, η_j varies from one type of labour to another. Nevertheless, η_j corresponding to k^o takes a unique magnitude.

DEFINITION 3.(Overall rate of surplus labour)

(42) $$\eta^{\dagger}(x^a) = \frac{1}{k^o(x^a)} - 1 .$$

It is easy to see that

(43) $$\eta^{\dagger} \leqq \eta_j .$$

That is, the overall rate of surplus labour is an extension of the minimum rate of surplus labour in the closed Leontief economy. Note that unless $\eta^{\dagger} = \eta_j$ for $\forall j$, $\eta_j > 0$ for some j, even if $k^o = 1$.

In the next stage, consider the dual problem of (LP.I). It is described as: (LP.II)

(44) $$\text{Max} \left\{ \Lambda F N^a \;\middle|\; \begin{array}{l} \Lambda B \leq \Lambda A + \gamma L , \\ \gamma N^a \leq 1 , \quad \Lambda \geqq 0_q , \quad \gamma \geqq 0_s . \end{array} \right\}$$

Since (LP.I) has optimum solutions, so does (LP.II). Let Λ^o and γ^o stand for optimum solutions of (LP.II). These two define:

Λ^o : optimum value vector,

γ^o : optimum reduction ratio vector.

Since (LP.I) means the maximisation of labour productivity, to call the optimum solutions of (LP.II) as in the above way makes sense. Note that, however, Λ^o and γ^o are normalized by N^a. [6)]

The amount of surplus value can be measured by Λ^o and γ^o. As the values of net products and the total wages are determined respectively by $\Lambda^o(B-A)x^a$ and $\gamma^o FN^a$, it follows that

$$\text{surplus value} = \Lambda^o(B-A)x^a - \gamma^o FN^a .$$

Hence, the *overall rate of surplus value* may be defined by

$$\mu^\dagger = \frac{\Lambda^o(B-A)x^a}{\Lambda^o FN^a} - 1 , \tag{45}$$

and the individual rates of surplus value by

$$\mu_j = \frac{\gamma^o_j}{\Lambda^o F^j} - 1 . \tag{46}$$

As for the relationship between $\eta^\dagger$ and $\mu^\dagger$, one has, as Proposition IV-2, the following:

PROPOSITION 16. $\eta^\dagger \geqq \mu^\dagger$.

Proof.

In fact, from (44), one has

$$\Lambda^o(B-A)x^a \leq \gamma^o I x^a \leqq 1 ,$$

and, in the light of Lemma 15(ii),

$$k^o = \Lambda^o FLx^a . \tag{47}$$

Hence, the conclusion is immediately derived. Q.E.D.

Since Λ^o and γ^o are not unique, $\mu^\dagger$ cannot be unique. The overall rate of surplus labour, however, is uniquely determined, and hence, may be regarded as a more relevant measure of surplus than the overall rate of surplus value. In a capitalist economy, $\eta^\dagger > o$ means exploitation.

It is evident that if labour is homogeneous, the above discussion will be reduced to that made in Chapter IV.

3. Is it possible to confirm the validity of the fundamental Marxian theorem in the closed von Neumann system?

For a given set of A, B, L and F, the von Neumann equilibrium is defined as follows. Consider

(48) $\quad \text{Min} \; \{\pi^w | p^w B \leqq (1+\pi^w) p^w (A+FL), \; p^w \geqq 0_q\}$,

(49) $\quad \text{Max} \; \{g^c | Bx^c \geq (1+g^c)(A+FL)x^c, \; x^c \geqq 0^n\}$.

As before, let p^w and x^c stand for the optimum solutions of (48) and (49) respectively, and π^w and g^c be the minimum and the maximum of the two respectively. These define the von Neumann equilibrium (π^w, p^w, g^c, x^c). Also write

$$M = A + FL \; ,$$

and make the following assumptions:

(B.4) $\quad B \cdot 1^n > 0^q, \quad 1_q M > 0_n.$

(B.5) $\quad \min \{ \pi^M \mid p^M B \leqq (1+\pi^M) p^M A, \; p^M \geqq 0_q.\} > o$.

The ensuing discussion will be developed as in the closed Leontief economy case.

Define the growth region as

$$G = \{x | Bx \geq (A + FL)x, \; x \geqq 0^n\} \; .$$

The greatest equilibrium growth rate can be defined as

(50) $\quad g^M(x^a) = \max \; \{g | Bx^a \geqq (1+g)(A+FL)x^a.\}$

PROPOSITION 17. $\eta^{\dagger} > o$ implies $\pi^w > o$.

Proof.

(α) If $p^w F = 0_s$, $\pi^w > o$ is guaranteed by (B.5).

(β) Suppose $p^w F \geq 0_s$. From (LP.I), one has

$$Bz^o \geqq Az^o + (1+\eta^{\dagger})FLz^o.$$

Premultiply both sides of this by p^w, and

$$p^w Bz^o \geqq p^w Az^o + (1+\eta^{\dagger}) p^w FLz^o, ,$$

whilst, postmultiplying (48) by z^o, one gets

(51) $\quad p^w Bz^o \leqq (1+\pi^w) p^w (A+FL) z^o$.

Hence,

$$\eta^{\dagger} p^w FLz^o \leqq \pi^w p^w (A+FL) z^o \; .$$

If $p^w FLz^o > o$, the conclusion soon follows. If $p^w FLz^o = o$, then $\pi^w > o$ follows from (51) and (40a): multiply (40a) by p^w, and then

$$(1+\pi^w) p^w Az^o \geqq p^w Bz^o \geqq p^w Az^o + p^w FN^a > p^w Az^o. \qquad \text{Q.E.D.}$$

PROPOSITION 18. (i) $G \neq \emptyset$ is equivalent to $g^c > o$.

(ii) $\eta^{\dagger}(x) > o$ is equivalent to $z^o(x) \in G$.

Proof.

(i) It is trivial that $g^c > o$ implies $G \neq \emptyset$. Conversely, if $G \neq \emptyset$, there exist $g > o$ and $x \geq 0^n$ such that $Bx \geqq (1+g)(A+FL)x$. Hence, by (50), $g^c = \max g > o$.

(ii) From (LP.I), one has

(52) $$Bz^o \geqq Az^o + \frac{1}{k} FLz^o.$$

If $z^o(x) \in G$, then there exists a $k < 1$, i.e., $k^o = \min k < 1$. Hence, $\eta^\dagger(x) > o$.

Conversely, $\eta^\dagger(x) > o$ suffices $z^o \in G$, for

$$Bz^o \geqq Az^o + \frac{1}{k} FLz^o \geq Az^o + FLz^o .$$ Q.E.D.

Now, for the sake of brevity, write

(53) $$\xi^c(x^c) = \xi(\Lambda^o(x^c), x^c),\quad \xi^a(x^a) = \xi(\Lambda^o(x^a), x^a),\quad \xi^*(z^o) = \xi(p^w, z^o(x^a)).$$

All these three magnitudes are finite and nonnegative. Then,

THEOREM VI. (Fundamental inequalities) (i) *(Growth constraint)*

(54) $$g^M \leq \frac{\mu^\dagger(x^a)}{1 + \xi^a(x^a)}.$$

(ii)
(55) $$\frac{\mu^*(x^a)}{1 + \xi^*(z^o)} \leq \pi^w \leqq g^c \leqq \frac{\mu^\dagger(x^c)}{1 + \xi^c(x^c)},$$

where $\mu^*(x^a) = \mu(p^w, x^a)$.

Proof.

Premultiply (50) by Λ^o, and one gets

$$(1+g^M)\Lambda^o(A+FL)x^a \leqq \Lambda^o Bx^a.$$

In view of (45), (54) is derived from this.

(ii) The first inequality follows, if (48) is postmultiplied by $z^o(x^a)$ and the result is rewritten in a relevant manner. From Proposition IV-3, $\pi^w \leq g^c$. The third inequality holds, if (54) is applied to the $x^a = x^c$ case. Q.E.D.

PROPOSITION 19. $g^c > o$ implies $\mu^\dagger(x^a) > o$ for $\forall x^a \in G$.

Proof.

From Proposition 18(ii), $g^c > o$ implies $G \neq \emptyset$. For $\forall x^a \in G$, one has $g^M(x^a) > o$. Therefore, $\mu^\dagger(x^a) > o$ from (54). Q.E.D.

THEOREM VII. (Fundamental Marxian theorem, generalised) $g^c > o$, $\pi^w > o$ and $\eta^\dagger(x^a) > o$ are all equivalent for $\forall x^a \in G$.

(This follows from Propositions 16, 17 and 19.)

Finally, one can show:

PROPOSITION 20. $\pi^w > o$ implies $\max_j \mu_j(x^a) \geqq o$. 7)

Proof.

Premultiply (49) by $\Lambda^o(x^a)$, and

$$\Lambda^o(x^a)Bx^c \geq (1+g^c)\Lambda^o(x^a)(A+FL)x^c ,$$

whilst, postmultiply (44a), with respect to x^a, by x^c, and

$$\Lambda^o(x^a)Bx^c \leqq \Lambda^o(x^a)Ax^c + \gamma^o(x^a)Lx^c .$$

Hence,

$$(\gamma^o(x^a) - \Lambda^o(x^a)F)Lx^c \geqq g^c\Lambda^o(x^a)(A+FL)x^c .$$

Since $g^c \geq \pi^w$, $Lx^c \geq 0^s$ and $\Lambda^o(x^a)(A+FL)x^c \geq o$, $\pi^w > o$ implies

$$\gamma^o(x^a) - \Lambda^o(x^a)F \nleqq 0_s ,$$

so that $\max_j \mu_j(x^a) \geqq o$. Q.E.D.

Thus, it is seen that similar propositions and theorems as in the closed Leontief system discussed in §§1-2 hold with minor modifications, even if heterogeneous labour is permitted in a von Neumann economy. Just as the discussion developed in Chapter I is generalised in Chapter IV, so is the discussion made in §§1-2 extended in §3. It is not difficult to point out the similarity or parallelism between the two generalisations.

4. How will skilled labour be reduced to unskilled labour in a von Neumann economy? This subsection will be devoted to making various remarks on how the discussion of this section would encompass the discussion made in §§1-2.

Consider a von Neumann economy which consists of dept.I and II: dept.I has n processes, exclusively producing m types of good , whilst dept.II, having r processes, is principally concerned with the production of skills. Note that dept.II is permitted to produce jointly both goods and skills, whilst dept.I is not. Let

B_1 m x n : output matrix of goods of dept.I,

B_2 m x r : output matrix of goods of dept.II,

B_3 s x r : output matrix of skills of dept.II,

A_1 m x n : input matrix of goods of dept.I,

J m x r : input matrix of goods of dept.II,

T s x r : input matrix of skilled labour of dept.II,

L_I s x n : labour matrix of dept.I.

Then, the output matrix of the closed system mirroring the sphere of value production is expressed by

$$B = \begin{pmatrix} B_1 & B_2 \\ 0 & B_3 \end{pmatrix} ,$$

and the input matrix by

$$A = \begin{pmatrix} A_1 & J \\ 0 & T \end{pmatrix} .$$

Likewise, the labour matrix is represented by

$$L = (L_I, 0),$$

whilst, the formal wage goods matrix is given, as before, by

$$F = \begin{pmatrix} 0 \\ I \end{pmatrix} .$$

As for the hyper-closed von Neumann system, one has

$$\tilde{B} = \begin{pmatrix} B & 0 \\ 0 & B_3 \end{pmatrix}, \quad \tilde{A} = \begin{pmatrix} A & 0 \\ 0 & T \end{pmatrix} , \quad \tilde{L} = (L, 0) , \quad \tilde{F} = \begin{pmatrix} F \\ 0 \end{pmatrix} ,$$

$$\tilde{\tau} = (0_m, 0_s, \tau) ,$$

where with respect to self-efforts, let us assume:

(B.1[2]) $\tau \geqq 1_s , \quad \tau_1 = 1 .$

Besides, similar notation will be employed, if necessary, so as to stand for the variables of the hyper-closed von Neumann system.

Now, since $\tilde{A}$ and $\tilde{B}$ are rectangular in general, it is hardly possible to extend (11) without alterations. Instead of an equality, it is necessary to consider an inequality as

(56) $(w, v, \gamma)\tilde{B} \leqq (w, v, \gamma)\tilde{A} + \tilde{\tau} .$

It is evident that the solution of this inequality system yields values of goods and labour power and reduction ratios in a generalised sense. The following two points, however, should be taken note of.

At the outset, Λ^o obtained in the previous subsections corresponds to (w,v) in (56), and γ^o is the counterpart of γ

in (56). Λ^o and γ^o are determined in the sphere of value production. In the next stage, therefore, self-efforts are disregarded in the previous subsections. The immediate purpose of this subsection is to make notes on these two points.

By applying the weak productiveness condition to the system described by $\tilde{B}$ and $\tilde{A}$, one has

PREPOSITION 22. The weak productiveness of the hyper-closed system is equivalent to the existence of nonegative solutions of (56):

$\exists\ x \geqq 0^{n+r}$ such that $(\tilde{B} - \tilde{A})x \geqq 0^{m+s} \iff \exists\ w \geqq 0_m,\ v \geqq 0_s,\ \gamma \geqq 0_s$ such that (56) holds.

Proof.

Put $W = \tilde{B} - \tilde{A}$, and Minkowski-Farkas' lemma (Lemma 14) can be applied to this system.

Q.E.D.

To state the problem precisely: first, (w, v, γ) satisfying (56) belongs to the set of the feasible solutions of (44), but is not necessarly its optimum solution. What is the condition that renders the solution of (56) an optimum solution of (44)? Next, the discrepancy between (56) and (44) is caused by the treatment of τ. What is its implication?

As for the first point, (44) is a subsystem of (56), with a more relaxed restriction. The optimum solutions Λ^o and γ^o of (44) satisfy (56), if

$$\gamma^o(B_3 - T) \leqq \tau$$

holds. A comparatively small B_3-T suffices for this.

With respect to the second point, one should point out that values and reduction ratios are determined by (44) from the angle of the maximisation of the productivity of labour, and that self-efforts hardly matter therein, because the maximisation of the productivity of labour can be taken into account within the sphere of value production alone. In the dimension of value production, the process transmitting value-creating force is latent.

Furthermore, in so far as the objective function of (44) is concerned, it may be said that the value of labour-power formally determines the reduction ratio.

If the discussion in this section (§3) is applied to a closed Leontief economy, one has

$$\Lambda^o = \gamma L(I-A)^{-1},$$

and

$$\gamma L x^a = 1 ,$$

to which

$$\gamma(I-T) = \tau$$

seems to be merely appurtenant.

That is, in a Leontief economy, the determination of value and reduction ratios by the maximisation of the productivity of labour coincides with that by the system of equations because of $(I-T)^{-1} \geqq 0$. In a von Neumann economy, however, the coincidence of the two becomes again impossible in general, as was discussed in Chapter III.

Nevertheless, even if self-efforts are in eclipse, the fundamental Marxian theorem still holds true, as established in this section, in explainging the quality of production and distribution.[8)]

§ 4. Concluding remarks -- On other discussions.

1. This section is concerned with critical comments on discussions made by some other economists.

Steedman argued about the reduction problem as part of his criticism of Marx. (Steedman [4], Ch. 7.) Let there be N types of heterogeneous labour, with w^j and ℓ^i standing respectively for the wage vector per unit of labour j and the vector of the amounts of labour i directly or indirectly necessary for the production of various types of goods. Define $V = (v_{ij})$, where $v_{ij} = \ell^i \cdot w^j$. Let

$$L = {}^t(\ell^1, \ldots, \ell^N) \geqq 0 \text{ ; } W = (w^1, \ldots, w^N) \geqq 0 ,$$

and one has

$$V = LW \geqq 0 .$$

For simplicity's sake, assume that V is indecomposable.

First, that $VE < E$ holding true for employment E means that surplus labour exists. A necessary and sufficient condition for this is that V is productive, i.e., $(I-A)^{-1} \geqq 0$. Surplus labour is seen to exist without the reduction of heterogeneous labour.

Secondly, let M and a_i, $i=1,..,N$, stand for an input coefficient matrix and a (direct) labour input vector respectively. Production prices p^m and the profit rate r are determined by

$$p^m = (1+r)p^m(M + \sum_j w_j \cdot a_j) ,$$

again without the reduction of heterogeneous labour.

In short, Steedman's conclusion is that the reduction of heterogeneous labour is redundant.

The above two points are a straightforward extension of his criticism of Marx as mentioned in Chapter I. That is, the first point corresponds to the fundamental duality, whilst the second is of the same type with the argument that the production price system in general can be determined by technical conditions and distribution.

The necessity of the concepts of value and reduction should not be sought in whether the production price system depends on value or reduction immediately and quantitatively: their significance resides in the understanding of the positivity of the profit rate and the growth constraint. Steedman's criticism of Marx here does not invalidate Marx's theory of value.

2. Bowles and Gintis approached the fundamental Marxian theorem with heterogeneous labour from a different viewpoint. (Bowles-Gintis [1], [2].)

Let C and L denote an input matrix and a labour matrix respectively. Introduce $\Lambda = (\lambda_{ri})$, where λ_{ri} stands for the amount of labour r required to produce one unit of goods i. Λ is determined by the following equation:

$$\Lambda = \Lambda C + L = L(I-C)^{-1}.$$

Let B and y be a wage goods matrix and an output vector respectively, and $(I-\Lambda B)Ly$ represents surplus labour. Note that $V = \Lambda B = (v_{rj})$ here is identical with Steedman's V .

From the above, the rate of exploitation can be defined by

$$\sigma(y)=\frac{(I-V)Ly}{vLy} \quad ,$$

and, for an individual type of labour,

$$e_r(y)= (1-\tilde{v}_r)/\tilde{v}_r \ ,$$

where $\tilde{v}_r = \sum_{i.s}\lambda_{si}b_{ir}$.

Bowles-Gintis discussed the relationship between the profit rate and these ratios, which are defined without the reduction of heterogenous labour, within the framework of a Leontief economy. The propositions derived from their argument are specialised cases of Propositions 11, 20, and Theorem VII proved in this Chapter.[8)]

Bowles-Gintis neglected the significance of the ratio expressed by $\{(Ly)_j/(vLy)_j\} - 1$ as a measure of exploitation, but this ratio corresponds to the rate of surplus labour in our previous discussion, and hence it would be irrelevant to disregard it.

3. The above two types of argument eventually ascribe the possibility of surplus labour to a property of the matrix, the components of which represent the amount of goods workers obtain, as Steedman's and Bowles-Gintis' V .

U.Krause (1) gave a thorough and formal argument on this point by introducing the standard reduction ratio.

Let A (n x n), L (m x n) and F (n x m) stand for an input matrix, a labour matrix and a wage goods matrix respectively. Production prices $p \geqq 0_n$ and the profit rate are determined by

$$p = (1+r)pM \ , \quad r = \{1/\rho(M)\}- 1 \ ,$$

where $M = A+FL$, $A \geqq 0$, $F \geqq 0$, and $L \geqq 0$.

Assume the economy is productive: $(I-A)^{-1} \geqq 0$. And, $H \geqq 0$, $H = L(I-A)^{-1}F$, (i,j) component of which represents the amount of labour i necessary to produce a unit of labour j. The *standard reduction ratio* is defined by α^* satisfying

(57) $$\alpha^*H = \rho(H)\alpha^* \ .$$

The rate of surplus value is defined by

(58) $$m(\alpha,y)= \frac{\alpha y - \alpha Hy}{\alpha Hy}$$

for $\alpha \in {}^m\mathbf{R}$ and $y \in \mathbf{R}^m$. Then, Krause showed:

Krause's Proposition. Assume A is indecomposable, $1_m L > 0^n$ and $1_n B > 0^m$. For $y \geq 0^m$ such that $\alpha^* y > o$,

(i) $r > o$, if and only if $m(\alpha^*, y) > o$.

(ii) $r > o$ implies $r \leq m(\alpha^*, y)$. [9)]

Proof.

(i) From (57) and (58), one has $m(\alpha^*, y) = \{1-\rho(H)\}/\rho(H)$. Let us show $\rho(M) < 1$, if and only if $\rho(H) < 1$.

Now, if $\rho(M) < 1$, then $\exists\, p \geqq 0_m$: $p > pFL(I-A)^{-1}$, i.e., $pF > pFL(I-A)^{-1}F = pFH$. Hence, $\rho(H) < 1$.

Conversely, if $\rho(H) < 1$, then $\exists\, p > 0_m$: $p > pH$, i.e., $pL > pHL$. It follows that

$$pL + pL(I-A)^{-1}A > pHL + pL(I-A)^{-1}A,$$

and hence,

$$pL(I-A)^{-1} > pL(I-A)^{-1}(A+FL) = pL(I-A)^{-1}M.$$

Since $pL(I-A)^{-1} > 0_n$ for $p > 0_m$, $\rho(M) < 1$.

(ii) First, put $U = (I-A)^{-1}FL$. Let us show $\rho(U) = \rho(H)$. As U and H play a symmetrical role, it suffices to show that $\rho(H) \leqq \rho(U)$.

It is trivial that $\rho(H) \leqq \rho(U)$, if $\rho(H) = o$. Assume $\rho(H) > o$, and $\exists\, x \geq 0_m$: $xL \geq 0_n$, and

$$xL(I-A)^{-1}F = \rho(H)x.$$

In view of $LU = HL$, one can rewrite this as

$$xLU = xHL = \rho(H)xL,$$

and hence $\rho(H) \leqq \rho(U)$.

Likewise, $\rho(U) \leqq \rho(H)$. Hence, $\rho(U) = \rho(H)$.

Next, let us demonstrate that $\rho(U) \leqq \rho(M)$, if $\rho(M) < 1$.

Now, $\exists\, y \geqq 0^n$: $Uy = \rho(U)y$. Since $I-M = (I-A)(I-U)$,

$$y - My = (I-A)(I-\rho(U))y.$$

From $(I-A)^{-1}FLy = \rho(U)y$, and $FL \geqq 0$,

$$(I-A)y \geqq 0^n$$

holds for $\rho(U) > o$.

If $\rho(U) \geqq 1$, then

$$y - My = (I-A)(1-\rho(U))y \leqq 0^n,$$

i.e., $\rho(M) \geqq 1$. In other words, $\rho(M) < 1$ implies $\rho(U) < 1$.

If $\rho(U) < 1$, then

$$y - My = (1-\rho(U))(I-A)y \leqq (1-\rho(U))y.$$

That is, $\rho(U)y \leqq My$, and hence $\rho(U) \leqq \rho(M)$.

Hence, if $\rho(M) < 1$, $\rho(H) = \rho(U) \leqq \rho(M) < 1$. Q.E.D.

The use of the standard reduction ratio validates the fundamental Marxian theorem for any output. Moreover, it is independent of the conditions in the market.

Let us apply the standard reduction ratio to the previous discussion made in §§1-2. In the closed Leontief economy, one has

$$H = L(I-A)^{-1}J(I-T)^{-1}.$$

Let w^* and v^* be the value of goods and the value of labour power corresponding to α^* respectively, and

(59) $$\alpha^*H = \alpha^*L(I-A)^{-1}J(I-T)^{-1} = w^*J(I-T)^{-1} = v^* = \rho(H)\alpha^* .$$

The following two points will be deduced from this: first, since H is the coefficient matrix which appeared in the evaluation of necessary labour, (17), α^* is also related to the rate of surplus labour: secondly, α^* as the reduction ratio equalizes the rate of surplus value to that of surplus labour, so that for all the types of labour the rate of surplus labour takes one and the same magnitude. This is a remarkable property of the standard reduction ratio.

Nevertheless, the standard reduction ratio can be defined in an economically adequate manner only in the Leontief economy case with $(I-A)^{-1} \geqq 0$.

4. It is Hollander(1) that tackled the fundamental Marxian theorem with heterogeneous labour by giving a different type of reduction ratio. He argued the validity of the fundamental Marxian theorem in the case that the reduction ratio is proportional to the wage rate. An extension of his argument will be examined here.

Consider a von Neumann economy as in §3, and make the same assumptions. Consider the following linear programming problem:

(LP.III)

(60) $$\text{Min } \{\psi L y \mid By \geqq Ay + FLx^a,\ y \geqq 0^n\} ,$$

where $\psi \in {}^s\mathbb{R}_+$. Since this has an optimum solution, let it be denoted by $y^o(\psi,x)$.

The dual problem of the above is described as (LP.IV):

(61) $$\text{Max } \{qFLx \mid qB \leqq qA + \psi L ,\ \ q \geqq 0_m\} .$$

Let $q^o(\psi,x)$ be an optimum solution of (LP.IV). In the light of the duality theorem, one has

(62) $$Ly^o(\psi,x) = q^o(\psi,x)FLx \ .$$

Define the *abstract rate of surplus labour* by

$$\sigma(\psi,x) = \frac{\psi Lx}{\psi Ly^o(\psi,x)} - 1 \ ,$$

and the *abstract rate of surplus value* by

$$\nu(\psi,x) = \frac{q^o(\psi,x)(B-A)x}{q^o(\psi,x)FLx} - 1 \ .$$

As before, one can derive

$$\nu(\psi,x) \leqq \sigma(\psi,x) \ ,$$

because one has (62) and the following from (LP.IV):

$$q^o(\psi,x)(B-A)x - q^o(\psi,x)FLx \leqq \psi Lx - q^o(\psi,x)FLx \ .$$

Besides, let the *individual abstract rate of surplus value* be defined by

(63) $$\nu_j(\psi,x) = \frac{\psi_j}{q^o(\psi,x)F^j} - 1 \ .$$

All the variables here depend on the parameter ψ . Then, how should it be specified? Hollander argued the case where $\psi = pF$, assuming the Leontief economy case.

Hollander's Proposition. Suppose $B = I$, and let the price system be determined by

(64) $$p = (1+\pi)p(A+FL), \ p \geqq 0_n .$$

(i) $\nu(\psi,x) = \sigma(\psi,x)$.

(ii)(Hollander) Suppose A is indecomposable and $\psi = pF$. $\pi > o$, if and only if $\nu(\psi,x) > o$. 10)

Proof.

(i) Since $q^o(\psi,x) = \psi L(I-A)^{-1}$ in this case, one has

$$\psi Lx = q^o(\psi,x)(I-A)x \ ,$$

and hence, $\nu(\psi,x) = \sigma(\psi,x)$.

(ii) Postmultiply (64) by $y^o(\psi,x)$, and premultiply (60) by p satisfying (64), and it follows that

$$\pi\{pAy^o(\psi,x) + Ly^o(\psi,x)\} = \sigma(\psi,x)\psi Ly^o(\psi,x) \ .$$

Since $(pA+\psi L)y^o(\psi,x) > o$ and $\psi Ly^o(\psi,x) > o$, $\pi > o$ is equivalent to $\sigma(\psi,x) > o$. From (i), the conclusion follows. Q.E.D.

Let us next extend Hollander's argument to a von Neumann economy. Only the conclusions are enumerated below. Employing the same notation as introduced in §3, one can show:

PROPOSITION 23.

(i) $$g^M \leqq \frac{\nu(\psi,x)}{1+\xi(q^o(\psi,x),x)} .$$

(ii) Assume $p^wF = \psi$. $\sigma(\psi,x) > o$ implies $\pi^w > o$.

(iii) $g^c > o$ implies $\sigma(\psi,x) > o$ for $x \in G$.

(iv) $\pi^w > o$ implies $\max \nu_j(\psi,x) > o$.

It should be remarked that $p^wF = \psi$ required in the above would hold provided that all the rows of F were to be proportional to each other. This may be the only case that justifies Hollander's argument. Therefore, the fundamental Marxian theorem suffers from this restriction in Hollander's context.

Moreover, (i) and (iii) do not hinge on the concrete specification of ψ . This fact is not peculiar, because surplus is invariably defined as a residue, which depends fundamentally on the necessary output or intensity.

5. By way of summary, some concluding remarks will be made.

In order to interpret Marx-Hilferding's reduction problem, three types of metamorphosis of labour should be clearly distinguished. On the basis of this distinction, it is seen that the industries producing ordinary goods are different from the education sectors, which produce skills, in the sense that different types of metamorphosis of labour are synthesised. The major difference is that in the former industries living labour is embodied as value in goods, whereas in the latter transference of value-creating force, i.e., living labour itself, takes place simultaneously with the production of skills, and hence living labour performed therein is not embodied as value. The education sector is the synthesis of value production, i.e., the production of skills, and the formative process, i.e., the transference of living labour. The specificity of the education sector is that in its labour process, i.e., in the formative process, the use-value of labour-power, i.e., living labour itself, is retained.

Based on our insight into the metamorphosis of labour, one can construct the closed system of value production and establish the system of equations to determine the values of goods and skills and the reduction ratios of skilled labour. It is also seen that the formative process is latent behind the backs of the producers. Note that the closed system is a decomposable system, but this does not create any difficulty in our discussion.

Formation of skilled labour is the accumulation of self-efforts which are exerted by all the constituent members of society. The result of production is the outcome of collective labour exercised by all the workers, whether or not they contribute to production immediately. This result established by Theorem I is very important in Marxian economics, because it shows that self-efforts alone are the ultimate source of new value. It must be observed that by Okishio's or Rowthorn's reduction ratios one cannot establish this theorem.

On the basis of the above, the amounts of surplus from three different angles are seen to be equal, as shown by Theorems II and III, and Morishima-Seton's equality is also true, as shown by Theorem IV.

Once various types of labour are admitted, however, the fundamental Marxian theorem, Theorem V, suffers from the following constraint: the fundamental Marxian theorem is valid for the state of the economy lying in the growth region.

Nevertheless, the state of the economy outside the growth region can no longer be persistent, and accordingly the economy should return to the growth region.

Negative rates of surplus labour may be concomitant with the state of the economy outside the growth region. This may be construed as the exploitation of workers by workers, but the exploitation of workers by capitalists is then incomplete.

Shifting the focus from the Leontief to the von Neumann economy, one encounters again the difficulty of generalising the analysis in terms of equality. The problem should be formulated in terms of inequality from the angle of the maximisation of the productivity of labour. The fundamental Marxian theorem and related propositions nonetheless hold, as in the closed Leontief economy, thereby retaining the qualitative aspect of Marx's value theory.

In this sense, it can be reconfirmed that the Marxian theory of value is still germane to an understanding of the capitalist economy.

Anyway, no one exploits capitalists in the capitalist economy.

CHAPTER VI

FUNDAMENTAL ANALYSIS OF DIFFERENTIAL RENT

Introduction -- Problems.

Modern society is composed of various classes possessing different types of production factor, and each class obtains income corresponding to its factor of production. In Marx's economics, the source of income and its distribution among the two major classes are treated first: the form of income other than wages is called profit in general, and those who appropriate profit are called capitalists.

If attention is concentrated on the agricultural sector, it is seen that there is a class of landowners, from which capitalists rent a patch of land and cede part of their profit as rent. Marx wrote:

"Landed property is based on the monopoly by certain persons over definite portions of the globe, as exclusive spheres of their private will to the exclusion of all others." (III, p.615.)

Possession of land, or monopoly of land, constitutes a historical premise to capitalism, but landholding itself does not determine the economic value of landed property. The economic value of landed property in the capitalist economy depends on the various conditions of the economy.

Consider a capitalist economy in which landed property required for agriculture is monopolized by the landowner class. Not only in the industry sector but also in the agriculture sector, the capital-labour relationship is established. The capitalists in the agriculture sector are the capitalist farmers, employing workers to plough land and paying a certain amount of money determined by contracts to the landowners.

Since the purpose of capital is the production and appropriation of profit, the capitalist farmers also invest their capital and price their products in subjection to the law of value. These conditions of a capitalist economy determine the economic value of landed property, i.e., rent.

Landed property, or the natural forces and/or natural conditions represented by landed property, is not a product of labour, so that it is on no account the source of value or surplus.

Then, how will the economic value of landed property be measured? Compare a factory powered by a steam engine with another using a waterfall. Suppose that the same type of product of equal quality is produced by the two which apply the same production technique, except for the source of power, and that they are sold at the same price in the market. Then, the factory powered by the waterfall would be more economically favoured, provided that the waterfall itself were to be available for nothing. This factory will produce *surplus profit*, i.e., the portion of profit over the average profit, which is created by economising on the steam engine. However,

"The possession of this natural force constitutes a monopoly in the hands of its owner; it is a condition for an increase in the productiveness of the invested capital that cannot be established by the production process of the capital itself; this natural force, which can be monopolized in this manner, is always bound to the land." (III, p.645.)

Let the waterfall belong to a landowner, then

"(T)he surplus profit which arises from the employment of this waterfall is not due to capital, but to the utilization of a natural force which can be monopolized, and has been monopolized, by capital. Under these circumstances, the surplus profit is transformed into ground-rent, that is, it falls into possession of the owner of the waterfall." (III, p.646.)

What applies to land can also apply to other forms of natural forces and conditions related to production. Owing to differences in natural conditions an equal amount of capital may yield unequal results of production. This can be attributed to the fertility and location of land.

The fertility of land depends on the chemical composition of the soil of land, and is determined by chemical and mechanical developments in agriculture:

"Fertility, although an objective property of the soil, always implies an economic relation, a relation to the existing chemical and mechanical level of development in agriculture, and, therefore, changes with this level of development." (III, p.651.)

Therefore, the fertility of land is not a mere natural fertility, but an economic fertility.

The same consideration can be applied to the location of land. Fundamentally, it is the distance relationship between a plot of land producing a certain kind of good and the market. Hence, the location of land is also an economic location of land that depends on the development of the transportation system.

The part of capitalists' revenue which, owing to the monopolisation of landed property, must be ceded to landowners in proportion to differences in degrees of fertility and/or location under the production price system is called *differential rent.*

Landholding itself has nothing to do with the creation of the value-portion representing rent. Natural forces and conditions are not the source of surplus profit, but its natural basis. That is, landholding is

> "... not the cause of the creation of .. surplus profit, but is the cause of its transformation into the form of ground-rent, and therefore of the appropriation of this portion of the profit,..., the owner of the land or waterfall." (III, p.647.)

From the angle mentioned above, Marx developed his theory of differential rent. Although he made an expatiation with the help of many complicated numerical examples, the objectives of his analysis can be reduced to the two points: how differential rent is determined in accordance with the theory of production price, and how it is influenced by changes in the productivity of capital.

The purpose of this chapter is to apply a microscopic framework of analysis to Marx's theory of differential rent, and so clarifying the basic points of his discussion.

In §1, the determination of differential rent in the Leontief economy case will be discussed, which corresponds to Marx's analysis of the first form of differential rent.

Changes in differential rent caused by unequal productivities of capital, or the second form of rent, will be argued in §2.

It must be underscored that this chapter is limited to the fundamental problems of differential rent.

In what follows, the term "fertility" is regarded as the representation of the natural conditions which can be monopolized.

§ 1. Differential rent in a Leontief economy.

1. Consider a capitalist economy accompanied by private landholding. The economy is composed of three classes, namely, the capitalist, the working and the landowner class.

The economy is made up of industry and agriculture. The industry sector produces n types of product, while only a single type of good is produced in the agriculture sector. It is called, according to the tradition of political economy, corn.

Let there be s types of land, which will be called land 1, land 2, ... and land s. Land is indispensable for agriculture, but is not necessarily required by the industry sector. Hence, only the capitalists engaged in agriculture rent plots of land from the landowners.

The economy is supposed to be of the Leontief type, except for two points: (1) in agriculture, different types of technique can be applied to different kinds of land, and (2) agricultural techniques are not necessarily linear, where only a single kind of technique can be applied to each type of land. Namely, the choice of (nonlinear) techniques concomitant with the heterogeneity of land is permitted in agriculture. This type of economy is called a *Leontief economy with landed property.*

Now, the following notation will be employed:

A	$n \times n$	:	input matrix (from industry to industry),
d	$1 \times n$	:	input vector (from agriculture to industry),
a_o	$1 \times n$	:	labour vector of industry,
K^j	$n \times 1$	:	input vector of industrial goods on land j,
Q_j		:	input of corn on land j,
L_j		:	labour input on land j,
H_j		:	acreage of land j cultivated,
$H = \sum H_j$		:	total acreage of land cultivated,
X_j		:	produce of corn from land j,
X		:	total supply of corn,
F		:	wage goods bundle,
p_I	$1 \times n$	:	price vector of industrial goods,
p_a		:	price of corn,

π : profit rate,

ω : wage rate,

λ_j : rate of surplus profit,

K_j : amount of capital on land j,

$m_j = K_j/H_j$: amount of capital per acre of land j,

where $K_j = p_I K^j + p_a Q_j + \omega L_j$.

The production function is written as:

$$X_j = X_j({}^tK^j, Q_j, L_j; H_j) ,$$

where $X_j = o$ if $H_j = o$.

Now, let us introduce:

DEFINITION 1.(Differential rent) Differential rent is the difference between the produce obtained by the employment of two equal quantities of capital on equal areas of land. (III, p.649.)

Given p_I, π and ω, the production price of corn from land j can be written as

$$(1) \qquad p_a X_j = (1+\pi+\lambda_j)(p_I K^j + p_a Q_j + \omega L_j) .$$

The difference in the above definition can be evaluated as

$$p_a X_j/H_j - p_a X_i/H_i = (1+\pi)(m_j - m_i) + \lambda_j m_j - \lambda_i m_i .$$

Without loss of generality, one can put $\lambda_i = o$. If $m_j = m_i$ and $H_j = H_i$,

$$p_a X_j/H_j - p_a X_i/H_i = \lambda_j m_j$$

is obtained. Therefore, let us write:

$R_j = \lambda_j m_j$: differential rent on land j.[1)]

Then, the production price of corn from land j can be rewritten as

$$p_a X_j = (1+\pi)(p_I K^j + p_a Q_j + \omega L_j) + R_j H_j .$$

Thus, surplus profit is transformed into differential rent, which is at the same time rent per acre of land.

The whole system of equations to determine prices and distribution is now represented as follows:[2)] for $j \in \{1,..,s\}$,

$$(2) \qquad p_I = (1+\pi)(p_I A + p_a d + \omega a_o) ,$$

$$(3) \qquad p_a X_j = (1+\pi)(p_I K^j + p_a Q_j + \omega L_j) + R_j H_j ,$$

$$(4) \qquad R_1 \cdot\cdot\cdot\cdot R_s = o ,$$

$$(5) \qquad \sum X_j = X ,$$

$$(6) \qquad p_a = 1 .$$

Equation (2) defines the production price of industrial goods and (3) shows that in agriculture the following equality

total production = production price + rent

holds, whilst (4) indicates that at least one type of land has zero differential rent, so that the production price of corn is determined by (2) and at least one of (3) : next, (5) means that the total produce of corn should be equal to a given magnitude. Needless to say, (6) is the numeraire equation.

The system of equations, (2) through to (6), consists of $n+s+3$ equations in $n+2s+3$ unknowns, i.e., p_I, p_a, R_j, X_i, π and ω. If the values of s unknowns are given, the remaining unknowns are simultaneously determined.

In the ensuing discussion, the production programmes of the capitalist farmers, X_js, are assumed to be given. Then, equation (5) becomes redundant, so that the prices, the profit rate and rent are determined as functions of the real wage rate.[3)]

From the above formulation, it is seen that

(7) $$\lambda_j = R_j/m_j = R_j H_j/K_j \; .$$

That is, the rate of surplus profit on one type of land appears as the ratio of rent to capital invested in that land. To determine rent is to determine surplus profit, but the latter is more important, albeit latent. In order to see this, let us consider here:

$p_a^{(j)}$: individual production price of corn produced on land j,

where

(8) $$p_a^{(j)} = p_a - R_j H_j/X_j \; .$$

Then, one has

(9) $$p_a = \{1 + \frac{\lambda_j}{1+\pi}\} \, p_a^{(j)} \; ,$$

and the following is easy to show:

PROPOSITION 1. Assume $1+\pi > o$ and $p_a^{(j)} > o$. Then,

(i) $\lambda_j > \lambda_i$ is equivalent to $p_a^{(j)} > p_a^{(i)}$, $i \neq j$.

(ii) $p_a = p_a^{(j)}$ if and only if $\lambda_j = o$.

Thus, the ranked order of the rates of surplus profit is equivalent to that of the individuyl prices, which means that from the angle of the capitalist class the ranked order of fertility of land is expressed by that of the rates of surplus profit rate, λ_js.

Since m_j differs from one type of land to another, the ranked order of differential rent is not equivalent to that of the rates of surplus profit: $R_j > R_i \Leftarrow\not\Rightarrow \lambda_j > \lambda_i$. In this sense, the surplus profit is transformed into differential rent.

If $\lambda_j > \lambda_i$, then land j is said to be more fertile than land i. The ranked order of land from less fertile to more fertile land is called the *ascending order*, whilst the reversed order the *descending order*. Since λ_j is a function of the real wage rate, the ranked order of rent may undergo changes when the real wage rate is altered. Such a change will render a type of land which has not yielded rent rentable, and vice versa.[4)]

2. Now, suppose that the real wage is specified as

(10) $$\omega = (p_I, p_a)F .$$

Let us write

$$A^*(j) = \begin{bmatrix} A & K^j/X_j \\ d & Q_j/X_j \end{bmatrix}, \quad L(j) = (a_o, L_j/X_j) ,$$

and

$$M^*(j) = A^*(j) + FL(j) ,$$

where the subsequent assumptions are made:

(A.1) $A \geq 0$, $K^j \geq 0^n$, $d \geq 0_n$, $Q_j > o$, $X_j > o$, $F \geq 0^{n+1}$.

(A.2) $L_j > o$, $a_o > 0_n$.

(A.3) The matrix A is indecomposable.

Then, one can see that $A^*(j)$ is also indecomposable.(Cf.Lemma 4.)

The equilibrium with differential rent is defined as:

DEFINITION 2.(Equilibrium with differential rent) The equilibrium with differential rent is the state of the economy such as $\pi > o$, $p_I > 0_n$, $p_a > o$ and $R_j \geqq o$ satisfying (2) through tc (6) and (10) for $\omega > o$.

THEOREM I.(i) The existence of the equilibrium with differential rent is equivalent to

(11) $$\rho\left(M^*(k)\right) < 1 ,$$

with k defined by

(12) $$\lambda_k = \min \lambda_j = o .$$

(ii) $R_j = o$ is equivalent to

(13) $$\rho(M^*(k)) = \rho(M^*(j))$$

for $\forall j$, where k concerns (12).

Proof.

Since (ii) is trivial, only (i) needs to be verified.

Sufficiency: as seen from (11), there exist $\pi > o$, $p_I > 0_n$ and $p_a > o$ in view of Frobenius' theorem. From (12), one has $R_k = o$ and $R_j \geqq o$.

Necessity: since $p_a > o$ and $\pi > o$, one has

$$p_a^{(k)} \geqq p_a^{(j)}$$

in view of Proposition 1. If $R_j \geqq o$, then

$$p_a \geqq p_a^{(j)},$$

whilst, from (4), there exists $j \in \{1,\ldots,s\}$ such that

$$p_a = p_a^{(j)}.$$

Hence,

$$p_a = \max p_a^{(j)} = p_a^{(k)},$$

that is,

$$\lambda_k = \min \lambda_j = o.$$

It is obvious that $p_I > 0_n$, $p_a > o$ and $\pi > o$ implies (11).

Q.E.D.

Needless to say, this theorem is valid even if $\lambda_j = o$ holds for more than two j-s.[5)]

According to the Marxian interpretation, this theorem discloses that the positivity of differential rent depends ultimately on the profitability of the economy, (11): without profit, capitalist differential rent cannot exist. Since positive profit, as made clear by the theory of value and surplus value, implies exploitation of workers, the capitalist and landowner classes share common interests in the exploitation of the workers.

The following analysis will be confined to the case of equilibrium with differential rent. Let us assume:

(A.4) $$\exists k : \rho(M^*(k)) < 1 .$$

(A.5) $$\exists i, j : \rho(M^*(i)) \neq \rho(M^*(j)), \; i \neq j .$$

3. Let us refer to other forms of the ratio of rent. Let

o_j : rate of rent per output,

κ_j : rate of rent in kind.

The rate of rent per output is defined by the total rental divided by output:

(14) $$o_j = \frac{R_j H_j}{X_j} .$$

Next, the rate of rent in kind is expressed by total rental divided by price-output:

(15) $$\kappa_j = \frac{R_j H_j}{p_a X_j} .$$

It is easy to see that

(16) $$\kappa_j p_a = o_j .$$

Concerning the relationship among λ_j, o_j and κ_j, one has:

PROPOSITION 2. The ranked orders of λ_j, o_j and κ_j are all equivalent: $\lambda_j > \lambda_i \Longleftrightarrow o_j > o_i \Longleftrightarrow \kappa_j > \kappa_i$, $i \neq j$.

Proof.

The second equivalence is easy to see in view of (16); whilst, from (2), it follows that

$$p_a = p_a^{(j)} + \kappa_j ,$$

so that the first equivalence is obtained in the light of Proposition 2. Q.E.D.

This proposition confirms that the ranked order of the rates of rent is the fundamental one.

4. The necessary terminolgy will be introduced here.

If capital can obtain average profit by cultivating a type of land, the type of land is said to be *competible*, and if it is actually cultivated, it is said to be *competing*. A type of land which participates in the determination of the price of corn, namely, a type of land which is cultivated but does not yield rent, is called *marginal land*, and the technique applied to marginal land is called a *marginal technique*. A type of land which can yield rent is said to be *rent-*

able. Rentable land is also competible.

Now, let us consider changes in the profit rate in the case in which marginal land is replaced.

Suppose that marginal land j is replaced by land k somehow or other. This replacement can take place either in the ascending or descending order. If it occurs in the acsending order, land j will not be cultivated any longer, for it is less fertile than land k under the existing real wage rate; if it does in the descending order, land j will turn out to be rentable, and still competible.

Before and after such a replacement, the two systems of equations hold:

(17) $$(p_I, p_a) = (1+\pi)(p_I, p_a)M^*(j) ,$$

and

(18) $$(\bar{p}_I, \bar{p}_a) = (1+\bar{\pi})(\bar{p}_I, \bar{p}_a)M^*(k) .$$

THEOREM II. The replacement of marginal land in the ascending (descending) order increases (decreases) the profit rate: if

(19) $$p_a X_k < (1+\pi)(p_I K^k + p_a Q_k + \omega L_k) ,$$

then $\pi > \bar{\pi}$.

Proof.

From (17) and (19), it follows that

$$(p_I, p_a) \leq (1+\pi)(p_I, p_a)M^*(k) .$$

Hence,

$$\frac{1}{1+\pi} < \rho\big(M^*(k)\big).$$

Consequently, $\bar{\pi} < \pi$. (Cf. Lemma 5.) Q.E.D.

It must be observed, however, that nothing can be said about changes in the prices.[6)]

In the next stage, consider how the total rental varies in response to increases in the acreage of cultivation. Let

R	:	total rental,
ζ	:	average rate of rent,
μ	:	average rate of rent per acre,
K_j	:	amount of capital invested in land j,
K	:	total capital in agriculture,

where,

$$K_j = p_I K^j + p_a Q_j + \omega L_j,$$

$$K = \sum K_j .$$

The total rental is defined by

(20) $$R = \sum_j R_j H_j = p_a X - (1+\pi)K .$$

The average rate of rent is defined by the total rental divided by the total capital invested in agriculture:

(21) $$\zeta = \frac{R}{K} = p_a \frac{X}{K} - (1+\pi) .$$ [7]

And, the average rate of rent per acre is determined by

(22) $$\mu = \frac{R}{H} = p_a \frac{X}{H} - (1+\pi)\frac{K}{H} .$$

Assume here that the input-output proportions are constant, irrespective of the extent of cultivation: the proportion

$$X_j : K^j_1 : \cdots\cdots : K^j_n : Q_j : L_j : H_j$$

is constant, so that one can write

(23) $$\varepsilon^1_j = \frac{X_j}{K_j} , \quad \varepsilon^2_j = \frac{X_j}{H_j} , \quad \varepsilon^3_j = \frac{K_j}{H_j} ,$$

and one has:

PROPOSITION 3. Assume marginal land is not replaced.

(i) $\lambda_j > o$ implies $\frac{\partial R}{\partial K_j} > o$.

(ii) $\frac{\partial \zeta}{\partial K_j} > o$ is equivalent to $\varepsilon^1_j > \frac{X}{K}$.

(iii) $\frac{\partial \mu}{\partial H_j} > o$ is equivalent to $\varepsilon^2_j \underset{(>)}{<} \frac{X}{H}$ and $\frac{p_a}{1+\pi} \underset{(<)}{>} \left(\varepsilon^3_j - \frac{K}{H}\right) / \left(\varepsilon^2_j - \frac{X}{H}\right)$.

Proof.

(i) From (20), it follows that

$$\frac{\partial R}{\partial K_j} = p_a \varepsilon^1_j - (1+\pi) .$$

Since there exists an equilibrium satisfying (2) - (6) and (10), one has

$$p_a X_j > (1+\pi) K_j ,$$

so that $p_a \varepsilon^1_j > 1+\pi$; namely, one has $\frac{\partial R}{\partial K_j} > o$.

(ii), (iii). Likewise, the conclusions follow from

$$\frac{\partial \zeta}{\partial K_j} = p_a \frac{\frac{\partial X_j}{\partial K_j} K - X}{(K)^2} = \frac{p_a}{K}\left(\varepsilon_j^1 - \frac{X}{K}\right)$$

and

$$\frac{\partial \mu}{\partial H_j} = \frac{p_a}{H}\left(\varepsilon_j^2 - \frac{K}{H}\right) - \frac{1+\pi}{H}\left(\varepsilon_j^1 - \frac{K}{H}\right) .$$

Q.E.D.

The first result (i) means that if the production of corn is extended on a rentable and competing type of land, the total rental is increased. The second indicates that extending cultivation of land j increases the total rental, if the capital-output ratio of land j is greater than the average output-capital ratio. The third can be interpreted in a similar fashion.

Roughly speaking, the extension of cultivation of land j with above average fertility increases the total rental and the average rate of rent. This confirms one of Marx's conclusions:

> "So long as the price of grain remains unchanged because the yield on the worst, rentless soil remains the same; so long as the difference in the fertility of the various cultivated types of soil remains the same; ... *First*, the rental constantly increases with the extension of cultivated area and with the consequent increased capital investment, except for the case where the entire increase is accounted for by rentless land. *Secondly*, .. If we leave out of consideration the case in which the expansion takes place only on the rentless soil, we find that the average rent per acre (total rental divided by the total number of the cultivated acres) and the average rate of rent on the capital invested in agriculture (total rental divided by the invested total capital) depend on the proportions which the various classes of soil constitute in the total cultivated area; ... In spite of an increase ... in the total rental with the extension of cultivation and expansion of capital investment, the average rent per acre and the average rate of rent on capital decrease when the extension of rentless land, and land yielding little differential rent, is greater than the extension of the superior one yielding greater rent. Conversely, the average rent per acre and the average rate of rent on capital increase proportionately to the extent that better land constitutes a relatively

greater part of the total area and therefore employs a relatively greater share of the invested capital." (III, pp.666-7.)

5. Consider the extension of the cultivated area either in the descending or ascending order as specified in the following.

Suppose the ranked order of fertility of land is given by land 1, land 2,..., and land s: $\lambda_1 > \lambda_2 > \ldots > \lambda_s$. The cultivable area of each type of land is given by H_j. The extension of cultivation goes on in the subsequent way: in the case of the ascending order, the cultivation of the first one acre of land j+1 follows that last one acre of land j, thus from the first one acre of land 1 to the last one acre of land s ; whereas, in the case of the descending order, the cultivation of the first one acre of land j follows that of the last one acre of land j+1, and hence from the first one acre of land s to the last one acre of land 1.

Here, as a corollary of Proposition 3, one can confirm:

PROPOSITION 4. (i) $\lambda_j = o \implies \frac{\partial\zeta}{\partial K_j} < o$; $\lambda_j = \max \lambda_i \implies \frac{\partial\zeta}{\partial K_j} > o$.

(ii) $\lambda_j = o \implies \frac{\partial^2\zeta}{\partial K_j^2} > o$; $\lambda_j = \max \lambda_i \implies \frac{\partial^2\zeta}{\partial K_j^2} < o$.

Proof.

(i) The proof is trivial.

(ii) By a mathematical manipulation, one gets

$$\frac{\partial^2\zeta}{\partial K_j^2} = -\frac{2p_a}{(K)^2}\left(\varepsilon_j^1 - \frac{X}{K}\right) = -\frac{\partial\zeta}{\partial K_j}\cdot\frac{2}{K} .$$

Q.E.D.

Now, consider the ascending order case. While land 1 is cultivated, rent does not accrue. Once the cultivation is extended to land 2, rent accrues, and the total rental and the average rate of rent increase with the extension of cultivation. Since the replacement of marginal land does not take place, the quantity of capital can be measured by the same prices, so that one has the following Figure 1.

Next, in the case of the descending order, it is invariably on marginal land that the extension of cultivation takes place. Hence, as marginal land is replaced, the prices undergo changes: only within the range of the extension of cultivation on one type of land, can changes in ζ be traced. Figure 2 shows the graph of ζ in this case.

FIGURE VI -1.

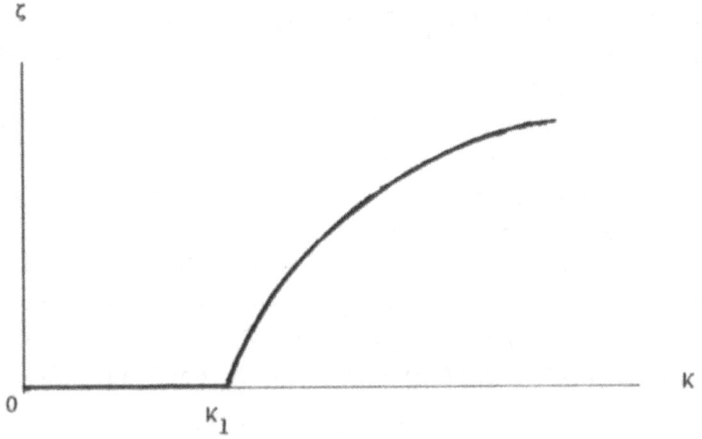

FIGURE VI -2.

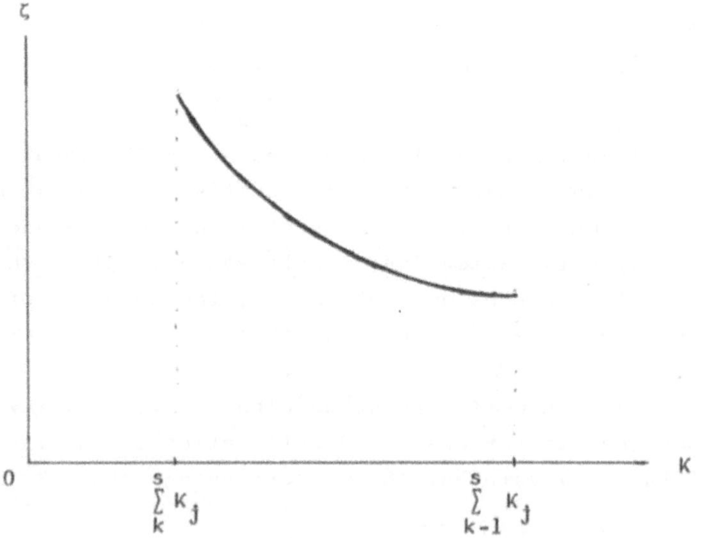

(Land k is being marginal.)

Note that in the light of Proposition 4(ii), one has the information about the slopes of the two curves drawn here. It is interesting that the curve in Figure 1 is increasing with decreasing gradients, whereas the other is decreasing with increasing gradients.

6. Let us briefly confirm here a classical proposition that there is an antagonistic relationship between the capitalist and landowner classes.

PROPOSITION 5. The rate of profit is a decreasing function of rent:

$$\frac{d\pi}{dR_j} > o .$$

Proof.

Take two vectors of rent, R^1 and R^2, and the price system can be written as

$$p^i = (1+\pi_i)p^iM + R^iH ,$$

where $i = 1 , 2$.

Suppose $R^1 \geq R^2$, and one has

$$p^1 = (1+\pi_1)p^1M + R^1H \geq (1+\pi_1)p^1M + R^2H .$$

Since M is indecomposable in view of (A.3), it soon follows that $\pi_2 > \pi_1$ in the light of Lemma 5. Q.E.D.

§ 2. The productivity of capital and differential rent.

1. The extensive cultivation of land invariably comes up against the natural limitation of the area of cultivable land, so that accumulation of capital should be shifted from the extensive to intensive form of agriculture. That is, capital accumulation should be carried on in such a way that an additional amount of capital is successively invested in the same plot of land. This becomes the fundamental form of capital accumulation in agriculture.

The productivity of capital may undergo changes as the accumulation of capital goes on, so that each unit of additional capital may yield unequal amounts of rent. Such an unequal result is called the second form of differential rent by Marx.

The second form of differential rent will be analysed on the basis of the first form of differential rent: namely, the principle that the production price of corn is determined by marginal land still applies.

Let the following notation be introduced: with respect to land j,

$K^j(i)$	$n \times 1$:	i-th investment of industrial capital goods,
$Q_j(i)$	:	i-th investment of corn,
$L_j(i)$	:	i-th expenditure of labour,
$X_j(i)$	:	i-th increment of output,
$\lambda_j(i)$	:	i-th increment of the surplus profit rate,
$R_j(i)$	:	i-th increment of the rate of rent,
$K_j(i)$	:	i-th increment of capital,

Obviously, one has

$$(24)\qquad \begin{aligned} K^j &= \sum_i K^j(i)\ , \quad Q_j = \sum_i Q_j(i)\ , \quad L_j = \sum_i L_j(i)\ , \\ X_j &= \sum_i X_j(i)\ , \quad R_j = \sum_i R_j(i)\ . \end{aligned}$$

Since additional surplus profit produced by additional investment is transformed into additional rent, one can write:

(25) $$R_j(i)H_j = \lambda_j(i)\{p_I K^j(i) + p_a Q_j(i) + \omega L_j(i)\},$$

and in view of

(7') $$R_j H_j = \lambda_j(p_I K^j + p_a Q_j + \omega L_j),$$

it follows that

(26) $$\lambda_j = \frac{\sum_i \lambda_j(i)K_j(i)}{K_j}.$$

That is, the rate of surplus profit is the weighted average of the additional surplus profit rates.

The second form of differential rent was defined by Marx as:

DEFINITION 3.(The second form of differential rent) The difference between the results which are obtained by the employment of equal amounts of capital successively invested in the same plot of land is called the second form of differential rent.

Let

$R^*_j(i)$: the second form of rent,

and, this is expressed by:

(27) $$R^*_j(k) = \frac{\sum_1^k \lambda_j(i)K_j(i) - \sum_1^{k-1} \lambda_j(i)K_j(i)}{\sum_1^k K_j(i) - \sum_1^{k-1} K_j(i)}$$

Soon, one can derive:

PROPOSITION 6. $$R^*_j(k) = \lambda_j(k).$$

That is, the second form of differential rent represents the change in the first form of differential rent given rise to by additional investment. It concerns the concept of the rate of change or marginal rent. Therefore, the analysis of the second form of differential rent will be reduced to the treatment of the changes in the first form of differential rent caused by alterations in the productivity of capital concomitant with additional investment.

In order to describe changes in the productivity of capital, the three usual cases, i.e., constant returns to scale, increasing returns to scale and decreasing returns to scale, will be considered: they are abbreviated respectively as c.r.s., i.r.s., and d.r.s.[8]

The production function will be rewritten as

$$X_j = f_j({}^tK^j, Q_j, L_j).$$

This is assumed to satisfy:

(A.6) f_j is partially differentiable, $\frac{\partial f_j}{\partial L_j} > o$, and $f_j \geqq o$.

(A.7) The proportion $t_K^j : Q_j : L_j$ is constant.

Note that changes in the productivity of capital reflect the accumulation of capital, in so far as they are engendered by it.

Now, the subsequent propositions are easy to show:

PROPOSITION 7. Assume that there is no replacement of marginal land, and $\lambda_j \neq o$. Then,

(i) If f_j is c.r.s., then λ_j is constant.

(ii) If f_j is d.r.s.(i.r.s.), then $\frac{\partial \lambda_j}{\partial K_j} \underset{(>)}{<} o$.

(iii) $$\frac{\partial p_a^{(j)}}{\partial K_j} \simeq -\frac{\partial \lambda_j}{\partial K_j} .$$

Proof.

(i), (ii). From (1), it follows that

$$K_j \frac{\partial \lambda_j}{\partial K_j} = p_a \left(\frac{\partial X_j}{\partial K_j} - \frac{X_j}{K_j} \right) .$$

Hence, the results are derived by dint of Lemma 18.

(iii) Likewise, one gets

$$\frac{\partial p_a}{\partial K_j} = \frac{-1}{1+\pi} \frac{\partial \lambda_j}{\partial K_j} .$$

Q.E.D.

From this proposition, it is seen that the rate of surplus profit, i.e., the rate of rent, increases (decreases) according as the productivity of capital increases (decreases) with the accumulation of capital. Needless to say, changes in the individual production prices are inversely proportional to those in the rate of rent.

The production price of corn is determined by marginal land: how does change in the productivity of capital invested in marginal land effect the profit rate? The following proposition concerns this:

PROPOSITION 8. Assume $\lambda_j = o$.

(i) If f_j is c.r.s., then π , p_I and p_a remain constant.

(ii) If f_j is d.r.s. (i.r.s.), then π decreases (increases).

Proof.

Since one has

$$\frac{\partial(K^j/X_j)}{\partial X_j} = \frac{1}{X_j}\left[\frac{\partial K^j}{\partial X_j} - \frac{K^j}{X_j}\right] \quad ,$$

it follows that

$$\frac{\partial A^*(j)}{\partial X_j} \gtreqless 0 \ ,$$

i.e.,

$$\frac{\partial \pi}{\partial X_j} \lesseqgtr 0 \ ,$$

according as f_j is d.r.s., c.r.s., and i.r.s. respectively.

Furthermore, if f_j is c.r.s., then p_I and p_a do not undergo any change. Q.E.D.

That is, if the productivity of capital on marginal land is kept constant, the production price system undergoes no alteration. An increase (decrease) in the productivity of capital, however, heightens (lowers) the profit rate. Note that in this case, nothing can be said about changes in relative prices.

As for the total amount of rental, the following holds:

PROPOSITION 9. Assume that marginal land (land k) is not replaced, and f_k is c.r.s. If f_j $(j \neq k)$ is c.r.s. or i.r.s., then

$$\frac{\partial R_j}{\partial K_j} > 0$$

Proof.

In the light of the assumptions made here, p_I , p_a and π are kept constant. From (3), it follows that

$$R_j H_j = p_a X_j - (1+\pi)K_j > 0 \ ,$$

and hence, if f_j is c.r.s. or i.r.s., then one has

$$H_j \frac{\partial R_j}{\partial X_j} = p_a \frac{\partial X_j}{\partial K_j} - (1+\pi) \geqq p_a \frac{X_j}{K_j} - (1+\pi) > 0 \ .$$

In view of Lemma 18, the result follows. Q.E.D.

Accordingly, if the production price system is kept unchanged, rent increases with the accumulation of capital in so far as the productivity of capital invested in rent-yielding land is not d.r.s.

The accumulation of capital will give rise to changes in the productivity of capital, and thus the ranked order of fertility of land and the production price system. Once marginal land is replaced, however, it becomes difficult to discuss changes in relative prices.

2. Suppose that each type of land is partitioned into several plots, and that different amounts of capital with unequal productivity are invested therein: land j, to which production function f_j is applied, is partitioned into m_j plots.

With respect to the α-th plot of land j , write:

$H_{j,\alpha}$	:	area
$K^{j,\alpha}$	n x 1:	input vector of industrial goods,
$Q_{j,\alpha}$	:	input of corn,
$L_{j,\alpha}$	:	input of labour,
$X_{j,\alpha}$	:	output of corn.

The production price system is now expressed as

$$p_I = (1+\pi)(p_I A + p_a d + \omega a_o) \quad ,$$

$$(29) \qquad p_a X_{j,\alpha} = (1+\pi)(p_I K^{j,\alpha} + p_a Q_{j,\alpha} + \omega L_{j,\alpha}) + R_j H_{j,\alpha} \quad ,$$

$$\sum_j \sum_\alpha X_{j,\alpha} = X \quad ,$$

where $j \in \{1,\ldots,s\}$, $\alpha \in \{1,\ldots, m_j\}$.

The system (29) consists of $n+3+\sum_1^s m_j$ equations in $n+3+s+\sum_1^s m_j$ variables. Suppose, as before, the production programmes of the capitalist farmers and the real wage rate are given, and hence (29c) is made redundant. Then, the production prices, the profit rate and rent are determined as functions of the real wage.

The following proposition concerns a necessary condition for equilibrium to hold:

PROPOSITION 10. If the system of (4), (6) and (29) has equilibria, then

$$X_{j,\alpha}/H_{j,\alpha} = X_{j,\beta}/H_{j,\beta} \quad ,$$

$$(30) \qquad K^{j,\alpha}/H_{j,\alpha} = K^{j,\beta}/H_{j,\beta} \quad ,$$

$$Q_{j,\alpha}/H_{j,\alpha} = Q_{j,\beta}/H_{j,\beta} \quad ,$$

$$L_{j,\alpha}/H_{j,\alpha} = L_{j,\beta}/H_{j,\beta} \quad ,$$

where $\alpha \neq \beta$.

Proof.

Since rent per acre is uniform throughout all plots of the same type of land, it follows that

$$(31) \qquad \frac{p_a}{1+\pi}\left(\frac{X_{j,\alpha}}{H_{j,\alpha}} - \frac{X_{j,\beta}}{H_{j,\beta}}\right) = \frac{K_{j,\beta}}{H_{j,\beta}} - \frac{K_{j,\alpha}}{H_{j,\alpha}} \quad ,$$

α, $\beta \varepsilon \{1,\ldots,m_j\}$, $\alpha \neq \beta$.

Suppose that neither of the two sides of (31) is zero, and one has

$$\left(\frac{X_{j,\alpha}}{H_{j,\alpha}} - \frac{X_{j,\beta}}{H_{j,\beta}}\right)\left(\frac{K_{j,\beta}}{H_{j,\beta}} - \frac{K_{j,\alpha}}{H_{j,\alpha}}\right) > o$$

in the light of $p_a > o$ and $\pi > o$. Then, the following is derived:

$$f_j({}^tK^{j,\alpha}, Q_{j,\alpha}, L_{j,\alpha}) > f_j({}^tK^{j,\alpha}, Q_{j,\alpha}, L_{j,\alpha}) \ ,$$

which is a contradiction.

Consequently, both sides of (31) are zero. Q.E.D.

This proposition shows that the establishment of equilibrium necessitates a uniform intensity of inputs per acre in each plot of the same type of land: the capitalist farmers renting the same type of land should adopt such production programmes as satisfy the uniformity of capital and labour intensity per acre.

Therefore, it may be said that in the long run the second form of differential rent does not exist persistently. As indicated by the system of (4), (6) and (29), the same type of land takes one and the same rent per acre, so that the second form of differential rent becomes a disequilibrium factor. Owing to the difference in the productivity of capital invested, a plot of marginal land, as pointed out by Marx, may yield rent, but it can come about only temporarily, because such a situation has the same effect as the replacement of marginal land in the descending order on the profit rate: if the productivity of capital invested in a plot of marginal land diminishes, the capital will be withdrawn from that plot and reinvested somewhere else.

Nevertheless, the establishment of equilibrium in the long run depends on the manner of contract between the capitalist and landowner classes, on any coalition of capitalists in an attempts to maximise the profit rate and on the divisibility of capital.

§ 3. A simplified case.

1. Consider a specialised case in which $n=1$. Then, all the coefficients in the system of (2) through to (6) are scalars. Let land 1 be marginal land.

The production price system of this case will be expressed as

$$(32)\qquad \begin{aligned} p_I &= (1+\pi)(p_I A + p_a d + \omega a_o)\ , \\ p_a X_j &= (1+\pi)(p_I K^j + p_a Q_j + \omega L_j) + R_j H_j\ , \\ R_1 &= o\ , \\ p_a &= 1\ , \\ \omega &= p_I F_1 + p_a F_2\ . \end{aligned}$$

Since p_I is a scalar in this case, changes in the relative prices can be discussed in relation to distribution.

Suppose that marginal land, land 1, is replaced by land 2 in the ascending order, and let $\bar{p}_I$, $\bar{p}_a$, $\bar{\pi}$ and $\bar{\omega}$ be respectively the prices, the profit rate and the wage rate after the replacement. Without loss of generality, one may put

$$X_1 = X_2 = 1\ .$$

The production price system after the replacement becomes:

$$(33)\qquad \begin{aligned} \bar{p}_I &= (1+\bar{\pi})(\bar{p}_I A + \bar{p}_a d + \bar{\omega} a_o)\ , \\ \bar{p}_a &= (1+\bar{\pi})(\bar{p}_I K^2 + \bar{p}_a Q_2 + \bar{\omega} L_2). \end{aligned}$$

Then, one can prove:

PROPOSITION 11. The replacement of marginal land in the ascending order heightens the relative price of the industrial goods.

Proof.

Before and after the replacement of marginal land, the following hold:

$$\begin{aligned} p_I &= (1+\pi)\left[p_I(A+a_oF_1) + p_a(d+a_oF_2)\right]\ , \\ \bar{p}_I &= (1+\bar{\pi})\left[\bar{p}_I(A+a_oF_1) + \bar{p}_a(d+a_oF_2)\right]\ . \end{aligned}$$

In the light of Theorem II, it immediately follows that

$$\frac{\bar{p}_I}{p_I} > \frac{\bar{p}_I(A+a_oF_1) + \bar{p}_a(d+a_oF_2)}{p_I(A+a_oF_1) + p_a(d+a_oF_2)}\ ,$$

from which one has $\bar{p}_I > p_I$, where $p_a = \bar{p}_a = 1$. Q.E.D.

The subsequent corollary is easy to show:

COROLLARY. The replacement of marginal land in the descending order lowers the relative prices of industrial goods.

2. In the next place, consider the case in which land 1 is not replaced, but the productivity of capital invested therein is i.r.s..

Suppose that capital is withdrawn from other types of land and reinvested in land 1, with the total output of corn kept unchanged.[9] Also suppose that the total quantities of capital in kind are kept constant. Then, a static comparative analysis can be applied.

Now, one has

$$M^*(1) = \begin{pmatrix} A+a_oF_1 & (K^1+L_1F_1)/X_1 \\ d+a_oF_2 & (Q_1+L_1F_2)/X_1 \end{pmatrix} ,$$

and, as X_1 increases, K^1, Q_1 and L_1 relatively decrease. Since capital is transferred to land 1 continuously, the elements of the second column of $M^*(1)$ change continuously, so that the rate of profit and the relative price of industrial goods also increase. continuously.

Write

$$K = p_I K^a + p_a Q + \omega L ,$$

where $K^a = \sum K_j$, $Q = \sum Q_j$, $L = \sum L_j$, $X = \sum X_j$.

Then, the following may be shown:

PROPOSITION 12. Suppose $p_a = 1$. Then, $\frac{d\zeta}{d\pi} < o$.

Proof.

From $\frac{dp_I}{d\pi} > o$ and $\frac{d\omega}{d\pi} > o$, it follows that

$$\frac{dK}{d\pi} > o .$$

Hence,

$$\frac{d\zeta}{d\pi} = -(p_a)\frac{X}{(K)^2}\frac{dK}{d\pi} - 1 < o .$$

Q.E.D.

Therefore, the profit rate and the average rate of rent are in an antagonistic relationship, which implies a conflict between the capitalist and landowner classes. Moreover, it appears that the wage rate goes up with an increase in the profit rate. This implies that real wages should go up if the relative price of industrial goods rises: the real wage rate does not change against the profit rate. However, this may imply the possibility of a coalition of the capitalist and working classes against the landowner class, as observed in the early stage of capitalism in England.

However, it should be remarked that the above proposition rests on the numeraire: if p_I or ω is taken as the numeraire, the antagonistic relationship cannot be observed. Thus, in general class relationships among the three classes are complex.

§ 4. Concluding remarks.

1. So far, fundamental problems of differential rent in the case where agriculture sector produces only one type of product have been discussed. By way of conclusion, some comments on further generalisation and the theory of value should be made.

In the first place, an extension to include more than two kinds of agricultural product should be contemplated.

Suppose that there are r types of agricultural good produced in agriculture. With respect to agricultural good i, produced on land j, write

K_i^j	$n \times 1$:	input vector of industrial goods,
Q_i^j	$r \times 1$:	input vector of agricultural goods,
$L_{j,i}$	:	labour input,
$X_{j,i}$	:	quantity of production,
$H_{j,i}$	:	area cultivated (acres),
D	$r \times n$:	input matrix of agricultural goods in the industry sector,
p_{II}	$1 \times r$:	price vector of agricultural goods.

The production price system is represented as:

$$
\begin{aligned}
p_I &= (1+\pi)(p_I A + p_{II} D + \omega a_o) , \\
(p_{II})_i X_{j,i} &= (1+\pi)(p_I K_i^j + p_{II} Q_i^j + \omega L_{j,i}) + R_j H_{j,i} , \\
R_1 \cdots\cdots R_s &= o , \\
\sum_j X_{j,i} &= X_i , \\
(p_{II})_r &= 1 ,
\end{aligned}
\tag{34}
$$

where $i \in \{1,\ldots,r\}$, $j \in \{1,\ldots,s\}$, and

$$X_{j,i} = f_{j,i}({}^tK_i^j, {}^tQ_i^j, L_{j,i}) .$$

The variables of this system are p_I, p_{II}, $X_{j,i}$, R_j, ω and π, i.e., numbering n+r+s+rs+2 in total, whilst the number of equations is n+r+rs+2. Hence, even if the production programmes of the capitalist farmers $X_{j,i}$ are given, the above system of equations (34) may not yield its unique solution.

In the system of equations here, the rent per acre instead should be treated as given. The system (34) then determines the prices, the profit rates, and the production programmes as functions of the real wage rate. This interpretation does not violate the fact that rent is surplus profit, and that the prices of agricultural goods are determined by marginal land.

A similar generalisation would also be possible in the von Neumann economy case. Assume constant returns to scale with respect to inputs of industrial and agricultural goods and labour input in agriculture, and the production price system can be described by:

$$pB^a = (1+\pi)(pA^a + \omega L^a) + RH^a, \tag{35}$$

together with (34c) and (34e), where

- A m x q: input matrix of the economy,
- B m x q: output matrix of the economy,
- R 1 x s: rent-per-acre vector,
- H s x q: input matrix of land,

and m=n+r, q being the number of processes in the economy, and A^a, B^a, L^a and H^a respectively represent the counterparts of the engaging processes.

Apply the von Neumann theory to (35), and it is easy to see that there exists an equilibrium, $p \geq 0_m$, $\pi > o$ for given $\omega > o$ and

$R \geq 0_s$, if the warranted rate of profit of the system (A,B,L) is positive. As shown in Chapter IV, this condition is satisfied if the rate of surplus labour is positive, so that the landowner class as well as the capitalist class depends on the exploitation of the working class.

It is also easy to see that in the system described by (35) the rate of profit is inversely related to each component of R. This implies, needless to say, an antagonistic relationship between the capitalist and landowner classes.

It must be remarked that these generalisations would never create difficulties in the theory of differential rent.

2. It must be observed that the theory of differential rent so far discussed does not immediately depend on the concept of value. Once the possibility of a positive profit rate is ensured by the fundamental Marxian theorem, the theory of differential rent may find its point of departure in the theory of production price.

Marx himself considered that the individual value of corn produced by rent-yielding techniques is smaller than that produced by a marginal technique, and called the difference between the two "false social value"-- false, because corn produced by rent-yielding techniques is regarded as having as great a value as corn produced by a marginal technique. Marx thus tried to establish the value-basis of rent.

It is not certain, however, that the individual value of corn produced by a marginal technique is greater or smaller than that by rent yielding techniques: in general, the ranked order of individual values of corn differs from that of individual prices. Therefore, it is not correct to explain rent in terms of false social value. Moreover, it is not necessary to do so: it is sufficient that rent is the part of profit ceded to landowners from capitalists.

This does not create, however, any difficulty in the theory of value. Value does not depend on the form of property ownership, but the production price system does, so that there exists a discrepancy between the two. The value concept should not be influenced by a concrete form of property, whether land or capital: the value system, whether in equality or inequality terms, will not undergo any change.

It is obvious that the value system which can apply even to the system discussed in §1 is the optimum value system, because the system comprises alternative techniques in the agriculture sector. And, it is also easy to see that the profit rate in that system, (2) through to (6) and (10), is the warranted rate of profit of the system.

It is important to reconfirm that the relationship between rent and profit concerns the redistribution of surplus value between the capitalist and landowner classes, and hence has nothing to do with the creation of surplus value. In their conflict against each other, rent becomes a barrier for the accumulation of capital in the sense that the profit rate will be pushed down.

EPILOGUE

By way of summary, some concluding remarks will be made.

In Chapters I through to V, we have discussed the Marxian value theory. We must emphasize that the value theory is not the price theory, but its basis.

As pointed out in Chapter I, the possibility of positive profit in the market cannot be explained by the market itself. The existence of production prices with a positive profit rate ensures this possibility. Furthermore, the existence of such a production price system is based on the positivity of the rate of surplus. We stress that although these reasoning are carried out in terms of equivalence, the Marxian value theory, the core of which is the so-called fundamental Marxian theorem, explains the foundation of the market in nonmarket terms. Note that even the existence of the production price system with positive profit does not depend on the market.

A superhistorical feature of the Marxian value theory, on which attention has been focused, is worthy of special reconfirmation, because the fundamental Marxian theorem explains profit in terms of something more general: to explain capitaism in terms of capitalism may not be relevant here. Thus, the foundation of exploitation is made clear.

Nevertheless, it is not necessary for detailed concepts which are introduced in the price system to have some explicit, microscopic value basis. The fundamental Marxian theorem is rather macroscopic, as is seen from the definition of the rate of surplus labour, and, as discussed in Chapter VI, a developed concept, such as rent, does not have a microscopic value basis, such as false social value.

To discuss more developed problems, such as the choice of techniques, dynamics etc., obviously means to go beyond the value theory. This task will be done in other places.

MATHEMATICAL ADDENDA

1. Quadratic systems with nonnegative matrices.

Let $A = (a_{ij})$ be an $n \times n$ nonnegative matrix.

Lemma 1. The following three conditions are all equivalent:

(i) $\exists x > 0^n : x > Ax$.

(ii) For $\forall y > 0^n$, $\exists x > 0^n : x = Ax + y$.

(iii) $(I - A)^{-1} \geqq 0$.

Remark ">" in (i) and (ii) can be relaxed to "≧".

Let $\rho \in \mathbf{C}^1$ and $\Theta \in \mathbf{C}^n$ satisfy

$$(\rho I - A)\Theta = 0^n,$$

and ρ is called an eigen-value of A, and Θ is called the eigen-vector associated with it. Since such a ρ can be obtained from $|\rho I - A| = o$, write

$$\Gamma = \{\rho \mid |\rho I - A| = o\} .$$

Lemma 2.((Peron=)Frobenius' theorem) There exists an eigenvalue $\rho^* \in \Gamma$ with the following properties:

(i) $\rho^* \geqq o$, $\Theta^* \geqq 0^n$: $(\rho^* I - A)\Theta^* = 0^n$.

(ii) $\dfrac{d\rho^*}{da_{ij}} \geqq o$.

(iii) $\forall \rho_n \in \Gamma$, $\rho^* \geqq |\rho_n|$.

(iv) If $Ax \underset{(<)}{>} \mu x$ for $x \geqq 0^n$, then $\rho^* \underset{(<)}{>} \mu$.

(v) $(\mu I - A)^{-1} \geqq 0$ if and only if $\mu > \rho^*$.

ρ^* and Θ^* above mentioned are called the *Frobenius root* and the (right-hand side) *Frobenius vector* of A respectively.

A matrix A is *indecomposable* if there exists no nonsingular matrix J such that

$$A = J^{-1}\begin{pmatrix} A_1 & * \\ 0 & A_2 \end{pmatrix} J ,$$

where A_1 and A_2 are square matrices.

Lemma 3. A is decomposable if and only if $\exists \rho \in \mathbf{R}$, $x \geq, \not> 0^n$: $Ax \leq \rho x$.

Lemma 4. Let $a \geq 0_n$ and $b \geq 0^n$. If A is indecomposable, then $A^* = \begin{pmatrix} A & b \\ a & c \end{pmatrix}$ is also indecomposable, where c is an arbitrary scalar.

Proof.

Suppose to the contrary. Then, there exist $\rho \geqq o$ and $\begin{pmatrix} X \\ x \end{pmatrix} \geq, \neq 0^{n+1}$, $x \geqq o$ such that

(*) $\qquad AX + xb \leqq \rho X \quad ; \quad aX + cx \leqq \rho x$.

If $x > o$, then from the supposition $\exists i: X_i = o$, but $X \neq 0^n$, because $X = 0^n$ implies $bx \leqq 0^n$ in (*a), which is impossible. Hence, $X \geq, \neq 0^n$. In view of $AX \leqq \rho X$ from (*a), A is decomposable.

Likewise, if $x = o$, then from the supposition $X \geq 0^n$, but $X \neq 0^n$ because for $\forall i: a_i > o$, $X_i = o$ in (*b). Hence, A is decomposable. This completes the proof. Q.E.D.

Lemma 5. Let A be indecomposable. There exists an eigenvalue $\rho^* \varepsilon \Gamma$ with the following properties:

(i) $\quad \rho^* > o$, $\Theta^* > 0^n$: $(\rho^* I - A)\Theta^* = 0^n$.

(ii) $\quad \frac{d\rho^*}{da_{ij}} > o$.

(iii) For $\forall \rho_n \varepsilon \Gamma : \rho_n \neq \rho^*$, $\rho^* > |\rho_n|$.

(iv) $\quad Ax \underset{(<)}{\geq} \mu x$ for $x \geqq 0^n$ implies $\rho^* \underset{(<)}{>} \mu$.

(v) $\quad (\mu I - A)^{-1} > 0$ if and only if $\mu > \rho^*$.

A nonnegative indecomposable matrix A is *stable*, if $\rho^* > o$ and

$$\lim_{t \to \infty} \frac{A^t}{(\rho^*)^t} = A^*$$

is finite.

Lemma 6. Let A be stable. Then, every column (row) of A^* is a positive column (row) eigenvector of A , both associated with ρ^*.

This lemma can be applied to the relative stability of a balanced-growth solution of the following homogeneous system:

$$z(t) = Az(t-1) ,$$

where A is stable, and $z(o) \geq 0^n$. For a particular solution of the system, $z(t) = A^t z(o)$, the following holds:

$$\lim_{t \to \infty} \frac{z(t)}{(\rho^*)^t} = A^* z(o) \quad .$$

The following lemma is also useful:

Lemma 7. Let $x \varepsilon \mathbb{R}^m$ and $y \varepsilon {}^m\mathbb{R}$. Then, the following two hold:

(i) $\qquad |I - xy| = 1 - yx$.

(ii) $\quad yx < 1$ is equivalent to $(I - xy)^{-1} \geqq 0$.

(Murata [2], pp.140-2.)

II. Equation systems with rectangular matrices and generalised inverses.

The following states a necessary and sufficient condition for the consistency (=solvability) of linear equation systems:

Lemma 8. A system of equations

$$A x = b$$

is consistent with respect to x, if and only if

$$\text{rank } A = \text{rank } (A,b) .$$

A generalised inverse concerns equation systems with rectangular matrices.

Definition. Let A be an $m \times n$ matrix. An $n \times m$ matrix X, which satisfies

$$AXA = A$$

is called a generalised inverse of A, and denoted as $X = A^-$. (Rao-Mitra, Definition 2.)

Lemma 9. $\{X \mid AXA = A\} \neq \emptyset$. (*op. cit.*, Lemma 2.2.3.)

Remark that A^- is not unique in general, and that the symbolic notation $A^- \geqq 0$ means that at least one possible generalised inverse of A is nonnegative. If A is square and nonsingular, A^- is reduced to A^{-1}.

Lemma 10.(i) A system of equations

$$A x = b$$

is consistent, if and only if there exists an A^- satisfying

$$AA^-b = b ,$$

in which case the general solution is represented by

$$x = A^-b + (I - A^-A)u ,$$

where u is an arbitrary m-column vector.

(ii) A matrix X is a generalised inverse of A, if and only if for all b such that $Ax = b$ is consistent, $x = Xb$ is a solution. (*op. cit.*, Theorem 2.3.1. and Corollary 1 of Theorem 2.4.1.)

Lemma 11.(i) $AA^-B = B$ is equivalent to $R(B) \subset R(A)$.

(ii) Let A be an $m \times n$ matrix, $AA^- = I$, if and only if rank $A = m$. (*op. cit.*, Lemma 2.2.4.)

Lemma 12. Let $Z = A + B$. If $R(B) \subset R(A)$ and $|I + A^-B| \neq o$, then, $(I + A^-B)^{-1}A^- \in \{X \mid ZXZ = Z\}$.

Proof.

Since $R(B) \subseteq R(A)$, it follows that $AA^{-}B = B$; and hence Z can be rewritten as

$$Z = A(I + A^{-}B) .$$

In view of $|I + A^{-}B| \neq o$, one can define

$$X = (I + A^{-}B)^{-1}A^{-} .$$

Those entail that

$$\begin{aligned} ZXZ &= A(I + A^{-}B)(I + A^{-}B)^{-1}A^{-}(A + B) \\ &= AA^{-}A + AA^{-}B \\ &= Z . \end{aligned}$$

Q.E.D.

III. Inequality systems.

Let A be an $m \times n$ matrix.

Lemma 13. (Stiemke's theorem) There exists an $x > 0^n$ such that $Ax = 0^m$, if and only if $\{p \mid pA \geq 0_n\} = \emptyset$.

Lemma 14. (Minkowski-Farkas' lemma) There exists an $x \geqq 0^n$ such that $Ax = b$, if and only if $pA \geqq 0_n$ implies $pb \geqq o$.

Note that this can be applied to the case where an inequality

$$Ax \leqq b$$

has a nonnegative solution. In fact, write $k = b - Ax$, and the inequality system is transformed into an equality system:

$$(A, I)\begin{pmatrix} x \\ k \end{pmatrix} = b .$$

An inequality system with a linear objective function is called the *linear programming problem.* Consider

$$\text{Max } \{cx \mid Ax \leqq b , \quad x \geqq 0^n\} ,$$

and this is invariably accompanied by its dual problem:

$$\text{Min } \{yb \mid yA \geqq c , \quad y \geqq 0_m\} .$$

Define

$$X = \{x \mid Ax \leqq b , \ x \geqq 0^n\},$$

$$Y = \{y \mid yA \geqq c , \ y \geqq 0_m\} .$$

If $X \neq \emptyset$, then the maximising problem is said to be *feasible.* The same applies to the minimising problem and Y.

Lemma 15. (i) If the two problems are feasible, they have optimum solutions: $X \neq \emptyset$ and $Y \neq \emptyset$ implies $\exists\, x^o \in X$, $y^o \in Y$ such that $cx^o \geqq cx$, and $y^o b \leqq yb$ for $\forall x \in X$ and $\forall y \in Z$.

(ii) (*Duality theorem*) $cx^o = y^o b$.

Lemma 16. If the maximising (minimising) problem is feasible and the objective function is bounded from above (below), the dual problem has a feasible solution: $X \neq \emptyset$, $cx < +\infty$, $x \in X$ implies $Y \neq \emptyset$. ($Y \neq \emptyset$, $yb > -\infty$, $y \in Y$ implies $X \neq \emptyset$.)

Lemma 17. The maximising problem has an optimum solution, if and only if the dual problem has an optimum solution.

IV. Miscellaneous.

Lemma 18. Let $y = f(x)$, $x > {}^m\mathbb{R}_+$, $y \in \mathbb{R}^1$ satisfy:

(*) y is partially differentiable, $\frac{\partial f}{\partial x_j} > o$, and $y \geqq o$.

(**) The proportion $x_1 : \cdots : x_m$ is constant.

Then, the following holds:

$$\frac{y}{x_j} \gtreqless \frac{\partial y}{\partial x_j}$$

and

$$\frac{y}{z} \gtreqless \frac{\partial y}{\partial z},$$

where $z = ux$, $u > 0_n$, according as $ty \gtreqless f(tx)$, $t > 1$ or $ty \lesseqgtr f(tx)$, $o < t < 1$.

Proof.

Since x satisfies (**), y is reduced to a function of one varialble. Without loss of generality, y can be regarded as a function of x_1. It suffices to show the proposition in the case of $y = f(x_1)$.

Now, suppose that $ty > f(tx_1)$, $t > 1$. Let

$$tx_1 = x_1 + \Delta x_1,$$

and $t \to 1$ is equivalent to $\Delta x_1 \to o$. Write

$$\Delta y = f(x_1 + \Delta x_1) - f(x_1),$$

and it follows that

$$\frac{\Delta y}{\Delta x_1} - \frac{y_1}{x_1} = \frac{x_1 f(x_1+\Delta x_1) - x_1 f(x_1) - \Delta x_1 f(x_1)}{x_1\, \Delta x_1}$$

$$< \frac{t x_1 f(x_1) - x_1 f(x_1) - \Delta x_1 f(x_1)}{x_1\, \Delta x_1}$$

$$= o .$$

Hence, assuming $\Delta x_1 \to o$, one has

(***) $$\frac{dy}{dx_1} - \frac{y}{x_1} < o$$

The other cases of the first are proved in the same fashion.

Likewise, z is a continuous function of x_1, so that x_1 is in turn a continuous function of z. Hence, y is regarded as a continuous function of z. Differentiate $z = ux$, and it follows that

$$\frac{dz}{dx_1} = u_1 + u_2 \frac{x_2}{x_1} + \cdots + u_n \frac{x_n}{x_1} = \text{const.}$$

This, together with (***), entails the second result. Q.E.D.

As for the details of the above, refer to Klein, Murata(1),(2), Nikaïdo and Rao-Mitra.

FOOTNOTES

Introduction

1) The terms, goods, products and commodities, are identical throughout the whole volume.

Chapter I.

1) Since inputs of production should come before outputs, there is a time-lag between input and output. If the production level differs from period to period, it may become difficult to evaluate the true inputs. In the above definition, therefore, the amount Ax is regarded as equivalents of inputs necessary for x, as if the state of the economy represented by x were to be repeated. This implies that some kind of steady state needs to be presupposed in the evaluation of net products.

2) The assumption (A.3) plays an important role in the discussion made in the Leontief economy case.

As for the indispensability of labour, (A.2) will be assumed in this chapter. Also see Chapter III, p.54.

3) It is also possible to consider reproducibility in a strong sense: for $\forall s > 0^n$, $\exists x \geqq 0^n$, such that $x - Mx = s$. Strong reproducibility, however, will be reduced to reproducibility, as is strong productiveness to productiveness.

4) This is designated as the average rate of profit by Marx. In this volume, the average rate of profit is identified with the equilibrium profit rate: they are referred to as simply the profit rate.

5) The production price is also the same as the long run equilibrium price, and is often referred to simply as price.

6) This type of production price was formally discussed by Sraffa in a systematic manner.

Let us note that in order to evaluate the profit rate the non-negativity of prices is not essential. It is derived from the exchange of equivalents in the market, in particular the payment of wages -- $pF \geqq o$: labour-power and wages are exchanged as equivalents.

7) Rigorously speaking, cost-price here is cost-value.

8) Morishima (5) contemplated the dual iteration of (23):

$$y^t = \frac{wy^{t-1}}{wMy^{t-1}} My^{t-1} ,$$

and showed that from any initial point $y^o \varepsilon \mathbf{R}^n_+$, the limit of the iteration, x^c , can be attained.

9) Consider $A = \frac{1}{4}\begin{pmatrix} 1 & 2 \\ 2 & 1 \end{pmatrix}$, $L = (1,1)$, and it follows that $w = (4,4)$. For an arbitrary $F = \begin{pmatrix} f \\ g \end{pmatrix} \geq 0^2$, the organic composition of capital of the two processes are equal: in fact, one has

$$wA = (3,3) ,$$

$$wFL = 4(f+g)(1,1) ,$$

so that $\xi = 3/4(f+g)$. However, it is easy to see that

$$|M| = \begin{vmatrix} \frac{1}{4}+f & \frac{1}{2}+f \\ \frac{1}{2}+g & \frac{1}{4}+g \end{vmatrix} \neq o .$$

10) Marx's original statement can be expressed as $dp_j/dw_j > o$. The economically typical case of this is that $p \propto w$. The former is more relaxed than the latter, but it is virtually more difficult to find its economically meanigful equivalent condition. This is why the latter is mostly discussed.

11) From the same reason as mentioned before in relation to net products (note 1) above), it may be also difficult to evaluate surplus products in a growing economy. At the end of period t, however, one can write

$$x_t = Mx_{t+1} + U_t ,$$

where U_t is the capitalists' consumption vector, because these exist at the same time point. If $x_t \propto x_{t+1}$ holds, moreover, this can be rewritten as

$$x_t = (1+g)Mx_t + U_t$$
$$= Ax_t + FLx_t + gMx_t + U_t ,$$

where g stands for the growth rate. Hence, the net products can be evaluated by

$$y_t = x_t - Ax_t ,$$

and the surplus products by

$$s_t = y_t - FLx_t .$$

That is, in the uniform growth case, the exact amounts of net and surplus products can be evaluated on the basis of the ongoing system of techniques. The time structure of production thus makes it difficult to evaluate net and surplus products.

Nevertheless, it must be noted that even if the economy is in a steady state and full information about techniques is given, the amount of surplus is obscured by the social system itself. This is what Marx tried to show in his value theory.

12) Differential rent, which is another form of income, will be discussed in Chapter VI.

Chapter II.

1) Fixed capital, durable capital and fixed equipment are regarded as being the same in this volume.

2) As for a simplified example of this reduction, see e.g. Schaik.

3) Koshimura [2] established an equation similar to (11) in the four departmental Marx-Leontief economy case, in which fixed capital, nondurable capital goods, wage goods and luxury goods are produced. He already knew that the "true" volume of amortisation should be evaluated on the basis of the growth rate.

Chapter III

1) This was produced from the equation (1') in Morishima (4), p.183.

2) Pd.C. is defined for Dx ">" 0^m in this chapter. The same note applies to Pf.C. and S.C. introduced later.

3) As for the generalised inverse, refer to the Mathematical Addenda, pp.147-8.

4) A Leontief economy in which alternative processes are permitted is usually called the generalised Leontief economy. Murata (2) discussed Marx's theory of value in the generalised Leontief economy case. Murata defined value as a minimiser of a certain type of norm, and the value equation is approximately solved by using Penrose's inverse. Penrose's inverse is unique, if it exists, and hence the value can then be determined uniquely. The value may rest on the form of norms, nevertheless.

5) The axiom of impossibility of land of Cockaigne means that the primary factors of production are essential for production, and hence it comprehends the indispensability of labour. Nevertheless, the two are tantamount to each other here, because labour alone is the primary factor of production in the present discussion.

As seen in Proposition 2, $L \geq 0_n$ does not suffice for the indispensability of labour.

6) This is an extension of the "efficient point" in activity analysis. Refer to Koopmans, p.60.

7) Kurz (2), in an attempt to criticise Steedman's counterexample, rewrites Steedman's value equation as follows:

$$5w_1 + \ell_1 = 6w_1 + w_2 ,$$

$$10w_2 + \ell_2 = 3w_1 + 12w_2 ,$$

where ℓ_1 and ℓ_2 stand for productivity indices.

From this, Kurz concluded that there exist ℓ_1 and ℓ_2 for which w_1 and w_2 are positive.

In Kurz's modified value equation, however, the same labour creates an unequal amount of value, and hence his assertion seems to be against the law of value.

8) A similar theorem was proved by Shiozawa (2).

9) Equation (22) will make no sense, if it is overdetermined. Hence, it may be plausible to presuppose $\operatorname{rank} H = \min(m, n)$, even if $m \leqq n$.

If $n < m$, (22) appears to be underdetermined: prices of $m-n$ types of good can be determined a priori. This, however, raises no difficulty in the present discussion.

10) If the iteration formulae (I-23) are immediately extended, one can write:

$$(23') \quad \begin{aligned} w^{t+1} B &= (1+\pi^t) w^t M, \\ 1+\pi^t &= w^t Bx / w^t Mx. \end{aligned}$$

Even if rank $B = m$ and hence $BB^- = I$, MB^- is not necessarily nonnegative.

11) The proof will be sketched as follows.

Repeat (23), and it follows that

$$(1^*) \qquad w^{t+1} = \pi^o \pi^1 \cdots \pi^t wQ^{t+1}.$$

Whilst, from Proposition 12, one has

$$(2^*) \qquad \pi^t = wQ^t Hx / wQ^{t+1} Hx,$$

so that

$$(3^*) \qquad \pi^o \pi^1 \cdots \pi^t = wHx / wQ^{t+1} Hx.$$

Substitute (3*) into (1*), and the subsequent equation holds:

$$(4^*) \qquad w^{t+1} = \frac{wHx}{wQ^{t+1} Hx} wQ^{t+1} Hx.$$

Here, wQ^t, which appears in (4*), is a solution of the following:

$$\xi^{t+1} = \xi^t Q.$$

Now, one can write

$$\lim_{t\to\infty} z_i^t / \xi_i^t = \gamma > 0,$$

where $z^t = wQ^t$, because $\xi^t = (\rho(Q))^t \theta(Q)$. (Refer to Lemma 6.)

From this, one can derive:

$$\lim_{t\to\infty} \pi^t = \lim_{t\to\infty} \frac{z^t Hx}{z^{t+1} Hx} = \lim_{t\to\infty} \frac{G\xi^t Hx}{G\xi^{t+1} Hx} = \frac{1}{\rho(Q)}.$$

Where, $G = (\gamma, \ldots, \gamma)$.

In the same fashion, one can prove

$$p^{**} = \lim_{t\to\infty} w^t.$$

Chapter IV.

1) Definition III-3 pertains to an arbitrary q, but the optimum value in this and the following chapters is restricted to that with respect to $y = FLx$.

2) The surplus value in Steedman's counterexample is negative, but Okishio(7) confirmed that even in that counterexample surplus products are produced. Also see Cheok, A. et al.

3) This naming seems to have appeared first in Krause(2).

4) The original definitions of the rates of unpaid labour and surplus value by Morishima are slightly different from (5) and (6).

Let there be N workers in society, and suppose their working day is T hours. Namely, one has

$$TN = Lx .$$

Let F^* stand for the wage goods vector per day. Then,

$$\text{the rate of unpaid labour} = \frac{T - \lambda^o_{F^*}}{\lambda^o_{F^*}} ,$$

$$\text{the rate of surplus value} = \frac{\lambda^o_Y - \lambda^o_{F^*N}}{\lambda^o_{F^*N}} .$$

Proposition 2 is valid for the rates of unpaid labour and surplus value defined above.

Note that in a different context Morishima's true value of good i will be of significance as an extension of employment multipliers, because it is unique.

5) Hollander(2) enumerated ten axioms and discussed the linearity of the measure of exploitation. The fundamental Marxian theorem, however, does not depend on the linearity of the valuations of goods.

Optimum value is, although nonnegative, neither unique nor linear. It may well be denounced for its nonoperationality.

Chapter V.

1) Note that when "skilled labour j" is mentioned, $j \neq 1$. Also remark that education and training necessary for skilled labour are regarded as being the same.

2) In Okishio (3), the counterpart of (2) is written as

$$\gamma = wE + \gamma T + \tau ,$$

(in the present notation). That is, the value of capital goods in the education sectors enters into the value-creating force of skilled labour. This, however, is incorrect as pointed out here.

3) As shown here, if the exclusive training period is considered, self-efforts become greater than unity. This is because self-efforts exerted in the education period are accumulated in worker j and reveal themselves when worker j starts working.

If it is the case that worker j works and studies simultaneously over his life, which is hardly possible in the actual economy, then the amount of self-efforts is exactly unity: one has only to put

$$n_{1j} = n_{2j} = n_j .$$

4) The following figure illustrates the accumulation of self-efforts to skilled labour.

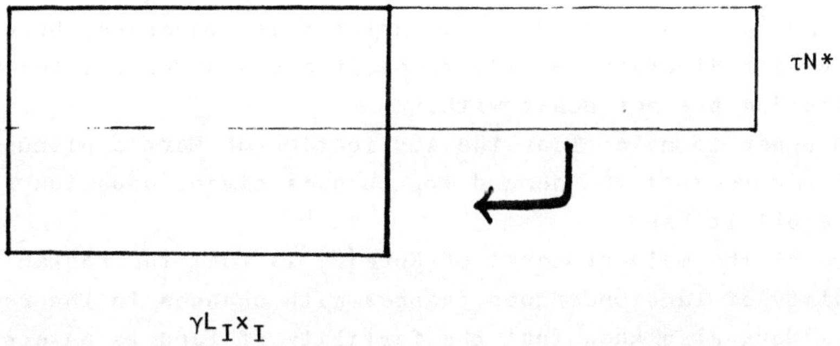

It should be taken note of that, as mentioned before, γ plays the role of a peculiar operator. Write, for instance $\tilde{x} - A\tilde{x} = \tilde{y}$ and premultiply (w, v, γ), and $\gamma y_{III} = o$, because no value is produced in the third sphere.

5) (L,T) in A does not give the labour matrix of the hyper-closed system, because T here is not related to the production of value.

6) Let $m = n = s = 1$, and all the variables and coefficients of (LP.I) and (LP.II) are scalars. Put $B = 1$, and one has $\Lambda^o = L/(I-A)N^a$ and $\gamma^o = 1/N^a$.

7) In a closed Leontief economy, one has a stronger result as $\max \mu_j > o$.

8) It will be convenient to make a note on the difference between the assumptions: $Lx^a \geq 0^s$ in §2 and $N^a > 0^s$ in §3. Since productive labour alone is conducive to the production of value, a strict inequality with respect to actual employment seems to create no problem. A similar distinction between productive and nonproductive labour, as made in the prpof of Proposition 10 can be applied to that of Proposition 17, if B , A , L and F are specified as in this subsection.

9) Krause's original theorem is proved for "$r \geqq o$". This proposition is a simplified version. For details, see Krause (1).

10) Hollander's original theorem is the conclusion (ii) here.

Chapter VI.

1) Differential rent is often referred to as rent in this chapter, because differential rent alone is discussed.

2) The production price system with rent of this type was first discussed by Sraffa, and later developed by Kurz (1), in which the two-land case is treated. His analysis is concerned, however, mostly with Ricardo. Marx's propositions and the existence of equilibrium are not dealt with.

3) In order to make clear the implication of Marx's discussion which assumes that the demand for corn is given, equation (4) is made explicit here.

4) One of the main concerns of Kurz (1) is that the ranked order of fertility of land undergoes changes with changes in the real wage rate. Marx also knew that the fertility of land is an economic fertility. See, e.g. the citation in pp.118-9.

5) Rent does not enter into the production price of corn immediately.

6) In his numerical examples, Marx often referred to rises and falls in prices, but, rigorously speaking, it is not easy to draw such a conclusion in the microscopic framework. See Proposition 12.

7) Marx's "rate of rent" is called the average rate of rent here.

8) See, e.g. Lancaster, p.131.

9) If the productivity of capital invested on fertile land is not d.r.s., this can occur.

REFERENCES

Abraham-Frois, G., Berrebi, E. (1979). *Theory of Value, Prices and Accumulation*, Cambridge Univ. Press.

Akyüz, Y. (1976). "A note on the Marxian transformation problem and income distribution," *Australian Economic Papers*, 16(1), pp. 96-108.

Baumol, W. (1) (1974). "The tranformation of values: what Marx 'really' meant. (An interpretation.)", *Journal of Economic Literature* 12(1), pp. 51-62.

———— (2) (1974). "Comment." *Journal of Economic Literature* 12(1), pp. 74-5.

Blakley, G., Gossling, W.F. (1967). "The existence, uniqueness and stability of the standard system," *Review of Economic Studies* 34(4), pp. 417-31.

Blaug, M. (1974). *The Cambridge Revolution: Success or Failure?* I.E.A.

Blundell-Wignall, A. (1976). "On exposing the transformation problem," *Australian Economic Papers* 16(3), pp. 277-88.

Böhm-Bawerk, E. von. (1896). *Zum Abschluß des Marxschen Systems*, in Sweezy (1).

Bortkiewictz, L. (1907). "Zur Berichtigung der grundlegenden theoretische Konstruction von Marx in dritten Band des *Kapital*," *Jahrbücher für Nationalökonomie und Statistik* 34(3), pp. 319-35. in Sweezy (2).

Bowles, S., Gintis, H. (1) (1977). "The Marxian theory of value and heterogeneous labour: a critiue and reformulation", *Cambridge Journal of Economics* 2(1), pp. 173-92.

———— (2) (1978). "Prof. Morishima on heterogenous labour and Marxian value theory", *Cambridge Journal of Economics* 2(3), pp. 311-4.

Brody, A. (1970). *Proportions, Prices and Planning -- A Mathematical Restatement of the Labour Theory of Value*, North-Holland.

Broome, J. (1977). "Sraffa's standard commodity". *Australian Economic Papers* 17(3), pp. 231-6.

Bruchman, G., Weber, W. ed. (1971) *Contributions to the von Neumann Growth Model*, Supplement 1 to *Zeitschrift für Nationalökonomie*.

Burmeister, E. (1968). "On a theorem of Sraffa", *Economica* 80, pp. 83-7.

Burmeister, E., Kuga, K. (1970). "The factor-price frontier, duality and joint-production", *Review of Economic Studies* 37, pp. 11-9.

Cheok,A., Davis,K., Harcourt,G.C. Maden,P. (1976). "Surplus value, profits and joint-production: Marx vindicated," (mimeographed).

Desai, M.(1979). *Marxian Economics*, Blackwell.

Dobb, M.(1)(1955). *On Economic Theory and Socialism*, Routlege and Kegan Paul.

——— (2)(1970). "The Sraffa system and critique of the neo-classical theory of distribution," *De Economist* 143, pp.347-62, also in Hunt-Schwartz, pp.205-21.

——— (3)(1973). *Theories of Value and Distribution Since Adam Smith*, Cambridge Univ. Press.

Eatwell, J.(1975). "Mr.Sraffa's standard commodity and the rate of exploitation," *Quarterly Journal of Economics* 89(4), pp.543-55.

Engels, F.(1895/96)."The role played by labour in the transition from ape to man," in Marx-Engels, *Selected Works* III, pp.66-77.

Fujimori, Y.(1)(1974). "Dynamic inter-sectoral balance models and Marx's scheme of reproduction," *Economia* (51), pp.47-71.(Yokohama)

——— (2)(1978). "The fundamental Marxian theorem with heterogeneous labour," *Economic Studies Quarterly* 29(3), pp.282-6.

——— (3)(1979). "Outputs, values and prices in joint-production," *Economia* (64), pp.61-87.

——— (4)(1980). "Sraffa in the light of Marx," *Josai Bulletin of Economics* 3(1), pp.61-73.

——— (5)(1981). "Formation of the Leontief core and the concept of pseudo-value," *Josai Bulletin of Economics* 4(1), pp.15-24.

——— (6)(1981). "Theory of value and joint-production," *Economic Studies Quarterly* 32(2), pp.156-65.

Fujimoto, T.(1979). "A comment on Takeda's note," *Economic Studies Quaterly* 30(3), pp.266-8.

Gale, D.(1960). *The Theory of Linear Economic Models*, McGrawHill.

Harcourt, G.C.(1972). *Some Cambridge Controversies in the Theory of Capital*, Cambridge Univ. Press.

Heertje, A.(1972). "An essay on Marxian economics," *Schweizerische Zeitschrift für Volkswirtschaft und Statistik* 108, pp.33-45, also in Howard-King(2), pp.219-32.

Heertje, A., Furth, D., Van Der Veen, R.J.(1978). "On Marx's theory of unemployment," *Oxford Economic Papers* 30(2), pp.263-76.

Hilferding, R.(1904). *Böhm-Bawerk's Marx-Kritik*, in Sweezy(1).

Hollander, H. (1)(1978). "A note on heterogeneous labour and exploitation," *Discussionsbeiträge zur Politischen Ökonoie* (14).

———— (2)(1979). "What remains of the labour theory of value? -- An axiomatic approach to Marxian exploitation theory." (mimeographed.)

Howard, M.C., King, J.E. (1)(1975). *The Political Economy of Marx*, Longman.

————(eds.)(2)(1976). *The Economics of Marx*, Penguin.

Hunt, E., Schwartz, J.G.(eds.)(1972). *A Critique of Economic Theory*, Penguin.

Klein, E.(1973). *Mathematical Methods in Theoretical Economics*, Academic Press.

Koopmans, T.C.(1951). "Analysis of production as an efficient combination of activities," Koopmans (ed.), *Activity Analysis of Production and Allocation*, Yale Univ. Press, pp.33-97.

Koshimura, S. (1)(1956). *Theory of Reproduction* (in Japanese),Toyo Keizai Shinpo Sha.

———— (2)(1967). *Theory of Crises and Waves* (in Japanese), Shunju Sha.

———— (3)(1975). *Theory of Capital Reproduction and Accumulation*, DPG Pub.

Krause, U. (1)(1981). "Heterogeneous labour and the fundamental Marxian theorem," *Review of Economic Studies* 48, pp.173-8.

———— (2)(1981). "Marxian inequalities in a von Neumann setting," *Zeitschrift für Nationalökonomie* 41(1/2), pp.59-67.

Kurz, H. (1)(1978). "Rent theory in a multi-sectoral model," *Oxford Economic Papers* 30(1), pp.16-37.

———— (2)(1979). "Sraffa after Marx," *Australian Economic Papers* 18(1), pp.52-70.

Lancaster, K.(1968). *Mathematical Economics*, Macmillan.

Lange, O. (1)(1963/71). *Political Economy* I, II, Pergamon.

———— (2)(1969). *Theory of Reproduction and Accumulation*, Pergamon Press.

Marx, K,(1965/67/59). *Capital* I, II, III, Progress Publisher.

Marx, K., Engels, F.(1969/69/70) *Selected Works* I, II, III, Progress Publisher.

Medio, A.(1972). "Profit and surplus value: appearance and reality in capitalist production," in Hunt-Schwartz, pp.312-46.

Meek, R.L. (1)(1956). *Studies in the Labour Theory of value*, Lawrence & Wishart.

———— (2)(1967). *Economics and Ideology and Other Essays: Studies in the Development of Economic Thought*, Chapman & Hall.

Morishima, M. (1)(1964). *Equilibrium, Stability and Growth*, Oxford Univ. Press.

———— (2)(1969). *Theory of Economic Growth*, Oxford Univ. Press.

———— (3)(1971). "Consumption-investment frontier and the von Neumann growth equilibrium," in Bruckmann-Weber, pp.31-8.

———— (4)(1973). *Marx's Economics -- A Dual Theory of Value and Growth*, Cambridge Univ. Press.

———— (5)(1974). "Marx in the light of modern economic theory," *Econometrica* 42, pp.611-32.

———— (6)(1974). "The fundamental Marxian theorem: a reply to Samuelson," *Journal of Economic Literature* 12(1), pp.71-4.

———— (7)(1974). "Marx's economics: a comment on C.C. Weizsäcker's article," *Economic Journal* 84, pp.387-91.

———— (8)(1976). "Positive profits with negative surplus va value: a comment," *Economic Journal* 86, pp.599-603.

———— (9)(1976). "Marx from a von Neumann viewpoint," in Brown et.al.(eds), *Essays in Modern Capital Theory*, North-Holland, pp.239-69.

————(10)(1978). "S.Bowles and H.Gintis on the Marxian theory of value and heterogeneous labour," *Cambridge Journal of Economics* 2(3), pp.305-9.

Morishima, M., Catephores, G.(1978). *Value, Exploitation and Growth*, McGrawHill.

Morishima, M., Seton, F.(1961). "Aggregation in Leontief matrices and the labour theory of value," *Econometrica* 29, pp.203-20.

Möschlin, O.(1974). *Zur Theorie von Neumannscher Wachstumsmodelle*, Springer.

Murata, Y. (1)(1977). *Mathematics for Stability and Optimization of Economic Systems*, Academic Press.

———— (2)(1977). "Fundamental Marxian theorem in case of multiple activities," *Metroeconomica* 29, pp.137-48.

———— (3)(1977). "Prices, rates of profits and dual stability in Leontief systems," *Economic Studies Quarterly* 28(2), pp.142-54.

Neumann, J.v.(1945/46). "A model of general economic equilibrium," *Review of Economic Studies* 13, pp.1-9.

Newmann, P.(1962). "A critique of Piero Sraffa, *Production of commodity by Means of Commodities*," *Schweizerische Zeitschrift für Volkswirtschaft und Statistik* 98, pp.58-75, also in Schwartz, pp. 346-62.

Nikaido, F.(1968). *Convex Structures of Economic Theory*, Academic Press.

Nobuta, T.(1977). "Sraffa and the structure of the invariable measure of value," *Review of Takushoku Univ.* (112), pp.81-140.

Nuti, D.M.(1977). "The transformation of labour values into production prices and the Marxian theory of exploitation," in Schwartz, pp.88-105.

Okishio, N.[1](1957). *Theory of Reproduction* (in Japanese), Sobun Sha.

——— [2](1963). "A mathematical note on Marxian theorems," *Weltwirtschaftliches Archiev* 91(2), pp.287-99.

——— [3](1965). *Fundamental Theory of Capitalist Economy* (in Japanese), Sobun Sha.

——— [4](1974). "Value and production price," *Kobe University Economic Review* (20), pp.1-19.

——— [5](1975). "Fixed capital and extended reproduction," *Kobe University Economic Review* (21), pp.11-27.

——— [6](1976). *Theory of Accumulation* (in Japanese), 2nd ed., Chikuma Shobo.

——— [7](1976). "Marxian fundamental theorem -- joint production case," *Kobe University Economic Review* (22), pp.1-11.

——— [8](1977). *Marx's Economics -- Theory of Value and Price* (in Japanese), Chikuma Shobo.

——— [9](1977). *Modern Economics* (in Japanese), Chikuma Shobo.

Okishio, N., Nakatani, T.(1975). "Profit and surplus labour: considering the existence of the durable equipments," (in Japanese), *Economic Studies Quarterly* 26(2), pp.90-6.

Pasinetti, L.L.[1](1977). *Lectures on the Theory of Production*, Macmillan.

———(ed.)[2](1980). *Essays on the Theory of Joint-production*, Macmillan.

Ricardo, D.(1951). *On the Principles of Political Economy and Taxation*, P.Sraffa ed., Cambridge Univ. Press.

Robinson, J., Eatwell, J. (1973). *An Introduction to Modern Economics*, MacGrawHill.

Roncaglia, A. (1)(1977). "Sraffa and price theory -- an interpretation," in Schwartz, pp.371-80.

———— (2)(1978). *Sraffa and the Theory of Prices*, John Wiley & Sons.

Rowthorn, B. (1)(1974). "Komplizierte Arbeit im Marxschen System," in Nutzinger-Wolfstetter (Hrsg.), *Die Marxsche Theorie und Ihre Kritik* II, Herder & Herder, pp.129-63.

———— (2)(1980). *Capitalism, Conflict and Inflation*, Lawrence & Wishart.

Rubin, I.I. (1972). *Essays on Marx's Theory of value*, Black & Red.

Samuelson, P.A. (1)(1957). "Wages and interest: a modern dissection of Marxian economic models," *American Economic Review* 47, pp.884-912, in *Colleted Scientific Papers* I.

———— (2)(1970). "The 'transformation' from Marxian 'value' to competitive 'prices': a process of rejection and replacement," *Proceedings of the National Academy of Sciences* 67(1), pp.423-5, in *C.S.P.* III.

———— (3)(1971). "Understanding the Marxian notion of exploitation: a summary of the so-called transformation problem between Marxian values and competitive prices," *Journal of Economic Literature* 9(2), pp.399-431.

———— (4)(1974). "Insight and detour in the theory of exploitation: a reply to Baumol," *Journal of Economic Literature* 12(1), pp.62-70.

———— (5)(1974). "Rejoinder: Merlin unclothed, a final word," *Journal of Economic Literature* 12(1), pp.75-7.

Schaik, A.B.T.M.v. (1976). *Reproduction and Fixed Capital*, Tilburg Univ. Press.

Schefold, B. (1980). "Von Neumann and Sraffa: mathematical equivalence and conceptual difference," *Economic Journal* 90, pp.140-56.

Schwartz, J.G. (ed.)(1977). *The Subtle Anatomy of Capitalism*, Goodyear.

Sekine, T. (1979). *The Dialectic of Capital* II, York Univ.

Seton, F. (1957). "The 'transformation' problem," *Review of Economic Studies* 25, pp.140-69, also in Howard-King (2), pp.161-76.

Shaikh, A. (1974). "Marx's theory of value and the so-called transformation problem," in Schwartz, pp.106-39.

Shiozawa, Y. (1)(1975). "Durable capital goods and their valuation," *KIER* 091, (Kyoto).

——————— (2)(1976). "Okishio's Marxian theorem generalised," *KIER* 096.

Sraffa, P.(1960). *Production of Commodities by Means of Commodities -- Prelude to a Critique of Economic Theory*, Cambridge Univ. Press.

Steedman, I. (1)(1975). "Positive profits with negative surplus value," *Economic Journal* 85, pp.114-23.

——————— (2)(1976). "Positive profits with negative surplus value: a reply to Morishima," *Economic Journal* 86, pp.604-6.

——————— (3)(1976). "Positive profits with negative surplus value: a reply to Wolfstetter," *Economic Journal* 86, pp.873-6.

——————— (4)(1977). *Marx after Sraffa*, New Left Book.

Steedman, I., Hodgson, G.(1977). "Depreciation of machines of changing efficiency: a note," *Australian Economic Papers* 17(1), pp.141-7.

Sweezy, P.M. (1)(1942). *The Theory of Capitalist Development*, Monthly Review.

——————— (2)(1949). *Karl Marx and the Close of His System & Böhm-Bawerk's Criticism of Marx*, Augustus M.Kelly.

Takeda, S.(1978). "A note on the fundamental Marxian theorem," *Economic Studies Quarterly* 29(1), pp.67-76.

Weizsäker, C.C.v.(1973). "Morishima on Marx," *Economic Journal* 83, pp.1245-54.

Weizsäker, C.C.v., Samuelson, P.A.(1971). "A new labour theory of value for rational planning through use of the bourgeois profit rate," *Proceedings of the National Academy of Sciences* 68(6), pp-1192-4.

Wolfstetter, E. (1)(1973). "Surplus labour, synchronised labour costs, and Marx's labour theory of value," *Economic Journal* 83, pp.787-809.

——————— (2)(1976). "Positive profits with negative surplus value: a comment," *Economic Journal* 86, pp.864-72.

Vol. 101: W. M. Wonham, Linear Multivariable Control. A Geometric Approach. X, 344 pages. 1974.

Vol. 102: Analyse Convexe et Ses Applications. Comptes Rendus, Janvier 1974. Edited by J.-P. Aubin. IV, 244 pages. 1974.

Vol. 103: D. E. Boyce, A. Farhi, R. Weischedel, Optimal Subset Selection. Multiple Regression, Interdependence and Optimal Network Algorithms. XIII, 187 pages. 1974.

Vol. 104: S. Fujino, A Neo-Keynesian Theory of Inflation and Economic Growth. V, 96 pages. 1974.

Vol. 105: Optimal Control Theory and its Applications. Part I. Proceedings 1973. Edited by B. J. Kirby. VI, 425 pages. 1974.

Vol. 106: Optimal Control Theory and its Applications. Part II. Proceedings 1973. Edited by B. J. Kirby. VI, 403 pages. 1974.

Vol. 107: Control Theory, Numerical Methods and Computer Systems Modeling. International Symposium, Rocquencourt, June 17–21, 1974. Edited by A. Bensoussan and J. L. Lions. VIII, 757 pages. 1975.

Vol. 108: F. Bauer et al., Supercritical Wing Sections II. A Handbook. V, 296 pages. 1975.

Vol. 109: R. von Randow, Introduction to the Theory of Matroids. IX, 102 pages. 1975.

Vol. 110: C. Striebel, Optimal Control of Discrete Time Stochastic Systems. III. 208 pages. 1975.

Vol. 111: Variable Structure Systems with Application to Economics and Biology. Proceedings 1974. Edited by A. Ruberti and R. R. Mohler. VI, 321 pages. 1975.

Vol. 112: J. Wilhelm, Objectives and Multi-Objective Decision Making Under Uncertainty. IV, 111 pages. 1975.

Vol. 113: G. A. Aschinger, Stabilitätsaussagen über Klassen von Matrizen mit verschwindenden Zeilensummen. V, 102 Seiten. 1975.

Vol. 114: G. Uebe, Produktionstheorie. XVII, 301 Seiten. 1976.

Vol. 115: Anderson et al., Foundations of System Theory: Finitary and Infinitary Conditions. VII, 93 pages. 1976

Vol. 116: K. Miyazawa, Input-Output Analysis and the Structure of Income Distribution. IX, 135 pages. 1976.

Vol. 117: Optimization and Operations Research. Proceedings 1975. Edited by W. Oettli and K. Ritter. IV, 316 pages. 1976.

Vol. 118: Traffic Equilibrium Methods, Proceedings 1974. Edited by M. A. Florian. XXIII, 432 pages. 1976.

Vol. 119: Inflation in Small Countries. Proceedings 1974. Edited by H. Frisch. VI, 356 pages. 1976.

Vol. 120: G. Hasenkamp, Specification and Estimation of Multiple-Output Production Functions. VII, 151 pages. 1976.

Vol. 121: J. W. Cohen, On Regenerative Processes in Queueing Theory. IX, 93 pages. 1976.

Vol. 122: M. S. Bazaraa, and C. M. Shetty, Foundations of Optimization VI. 193 pages. 1976

Vol. 123: Multiple Criteria Decision Making. Kyoto 1975. Edited by M. Zeleny. XXVII, 345 pages. 1976.

Vol. 124: M. J. Todd. The Computation of Fixed Points and Applications. VII, 129 pages. 1976.

Vol. 125: Karl C. Mosler. Optimale Transportnetze. Zur Bestimmung ihres kostengünstigsten Standorts bei gegebener Nachfrage. VI, 142 Seiten. 1976.

Vol. 126: Energy, Regional Science and Public Policy. Energy and Environment I. Proceedings 1975. Edited by M. Chatterji and P. Van Rompuy. VIII, 316 pages. 1976.

Vol. 127: Environment, Regional Science and Interregional Modeling. Energy and Environment II. Proceedings 1975. Edited by M. Chatterji and P. Van Rompuy. IX, 211 pages. 1976.

Vol. 128: Integer Programming and Related Areas. A Classified Bibliography. Edited by C. Kastning. XII, 495 pages. 1976.

Vol. 129: H.-J. Lüthi, Komplementaritäts- und Fixpunktalgorithmen in der mathematischen Programmierung. Spieltheorie und Ökonomie. VII, 145 Seiten. 1976.

Vol. 130: Multiple Criteria Decision Making, Jouy-en-Josas, France. Proceedings 1975. Edited by H. Thiriez and S. Zionts. VI, 409 pages. 1976.

Vol. 131: Mathematical Systems Theory. Proceedings 1975. Edited by G. Marchesini and S. K. Mitter. X, 408 pages. 1976.

Vol. 132: U. H. Funke, Mathematical Models in Marketing. A Collection of Abstracts. XX, 514 pages. 1976.

Vol. 133: Warsaw Fall Seminars in Mathematical Economics 1975. Edited by M. W. Loś, J. Loś, and A. Wieczorek. V. 159 pages. 1976.

Vol. 134: Computing Methods in Applied Sciences and Engineering. Proceedings 1975. VIII, 390 pages. 1976.

Vol. 135: H. Haga, A Disequilibrium – Equilibrium Model with Money and Bonds. A Keynesian – Walrasian Synthesis. VI, 119 pages. 1976.

Vol. 136: E. Kofler und G. Menges, Entscheidungen bei unvollständiger Information. XII, 357 Seiten. 1976.

Vol. 137: R. Wets, Grundlagen Konvexer Optimierung. VI, 146 Seiten. 1976.

Vol. 138: K. Okuguchi, Expectations and Stability in Oligopoly Models. VI, 103 pages. 1976.

Vol. 139: Production Theory and Its Applications. Proceedings. Edited by H. Albach and G. Bergendahl. VIII, 193 pages. 1977.

Vol. 140: W. Eichhorn and J. Voeller, Theory of the Price Index. Fisher's Test Approach and Generalizations. VII, 95 pages. 1976.

Vol. 141: Mathematical Economics and Game Theory. Essays in Honor of Oskar Morgenstern. Edited by R. Henn and O. Moeschlin. XIV, 703 pages. 1977.

Vol. 142: J. S. Lane, On Optimal Population Paths. V, 123 pages. 1977.

Vol. 143: B. Näslund, An Analysis of Economic Size Distributions. XV, 100 pages. 1977.

Vol. 144: Convex Analysis and Its Applications. Proceedings 1976. Edited by A. Auslender. VI, 219 pages. 1977.

Vol. 145: J. Rosenmüller, Extreme Games and Their Solutions. IV, 126 pages. 1977.

Vol. 146: In Search of Economic Indicators. Edited by W. H. Strigel. XVI, 198 pages. 1977.

Vol. 147: Resource Allocation and Division of Space. Proceedings. Edited by T. Fujii and R. Sato. VIII, 184 pages. 1977.

Vol. 148: C. E. Mandl, Simulationstechnik und Simulationsmodelle in den Sozial- und Wirtschaftswissenschaften. IX, 173 Seiten. 1977.

Vol. 149: Stationäre und schrumpfende Bevölkerungen: Demographisches Null- und Negativwachstum in Österreich. Herausgegeben von G. Feichtinger. VI, 262 Seiten. 1977.

Vol. 150: Bauer et al., Supercritical Wing Sections III. VI, 179 pages. 1977.

Vol. 151: C. A. Schneeweiß, Inventory-Production Theory. VI, 116 pages. 1977.

Vol. 152: Kirsch et al., Notwendige Optimalitätsbedingungen und ihre Anwendung. VI, 157 Seiten. 1978.

Vol. 153: Kombinatorische Entscheidungsprobleme: Methoden und Anwendungen. Herausgegeben von T. M. Liebling und M. Rössler. VIII, 206 Seiten. 1978.

Vol. 154: Problems and Instruments of Business Cycle Analysis. Proceedings 1977. Edited by W. H. Strigel. VI, 442 pages. 1978.

Vol. 155: Multiple Criteria Problem Solving. Proceedings 1977. Edited by S. Zionts. VIII, 567 pages. 1978.

Vol. 156: B. Näslund and B. Sellstedt, Neo-Ricardian Theory. With Applications to Some Current Economic Problems. VI, 165 pages. 1978.

Vol. 157: Optimization and Operations Research. Proceedings 1977. Edited by R. Henn, B. Korte, and W. Oettli. VI, 270 pages. 1978.

Vol. 158: L. J. Cherene, Set Valued Dynamical Systems and Economic Flow. VIII, 83 pages. 1978.

Vol. 159: Some Aspects of the Foundations of General Equilibrium Theory: The Posthumous Papers of Peter J. Kalman. Edited by J. Green. VI, 167 pages. 1978.

Ökonometrie und Unternehmensforschung
Econometrics and Operations Research

Vol. I Nichtlineare Programmierung. Von H. P. Künzi und W. Krelle unter Mitwirkung von W. Oettli. Vergriffen

Vol. II Lineare Programmierung und Erweiterungen. Von G. B. Dantzig. Ins Deutsche übertragen und bearbeitet von A. Jaeger. – Mit 103 Abbildungen. XVI, 712 Seiten. 1966. Geb.

Vol. III Stochastic Processes. By M. Girault. – With 35 figures. XII, 126 pages. 1966. Cloth

Vol. IV Methoden der Unternehmensforschung im Versicherungswesen. Von K. H. Wolff. – Mit 14 Diagrammen. VIII, 266 Seiten. 1966. Geb.

Vol. V The Theory of Max-Min and its Application to Weapons Allocation Problems. By John M. Danskin. – With 6 figures. X, 126 pages. 1967. Cloth

Vol. VI Entscheidungskriterien bei Risiko. Von H. Schneeweiss. – Mit 35 Abbildungen. XII, 215 Seiten. 1967. Geb.

Vol. VII Boolean Methods in Operations Research and Related Areas. By P. L. Hammer (Ivănescu) and S. Rudeanu. With a preface by R. Bellman. – With 25 figures. XVI, 329 pages. 1968. Cloth

Vol. VIII Strategy for R & D: Studies in the Microeconomics of Development. By Th. Marschak. Th K. Glennan Jr., and R. Summers. – With 44 figures. XIV, 330 pages. 1967. Cloth

Vol. IX Dynamic Programming of Economic Decisions. By M. J. Beckmann. – With 9 figures XII, 143 pages. 1968. Cloth

Vol. X Input-Output-Analyse. Von J. Schumann. – Mit 12 Abbildungen. X, 311 Seiten. 1968. Geb.

Vol. XI Produktionstheorie. Von W. Wittmann. – Mit 54 Abbildungen. VIII, 177 Seiten. 1968. Geb.

Vol. XII Sensitivitätsanalysen und parametrische Programmierung. Von W. Dinkelbach. – Mit 20 Abbildungen. XI, 190 Seiten. 1969. Geb.

Vol. XIII Graphentheoretische Methoden und ihre Anwendungen. Von W. Knödel. – Mit 24 Abbildungen. VIII, 111 Seiten. 1969. Geb.

Vol. XIV Praktische Studien zur Unternehmensforschung. Von E. Nievergelt, O. Müller, F. E. Schlaepfer und W. H. Landis. – Mit 82 Abbildungen. XII, 240 Seiten. 1970. Geb.

Vol. XV Optimale Reihenfolgen. Von H. Müller-Merbach. – Mit 45 Abbildungen. IX, 225 Seiten. 1970. Geb.

Vol. XVI Preispolitik der Mehrproduktenunternehmung in der statischen Theorie. Von R. Selten. – Mit 20 Abbildungen. VIII, 195 Seiten. 1970. Geb.

Vol. XVII Information Theory for Systems Engineers. By L. P. Hyvärinen. – With 42 figures. VIII, 197 pages. 1970. Cloth

Vol. XVIII Unternehmensforschung im Bergbau. Von F. L. Wilke. – Mit 29 Abbildungen. VIII, 150 Seiten. 1972. Geb.

Vol. XIX Anti-Äquilibrium. Von J. Kornai. – Mit 31 Abbildungen. XVI, 382 Seiten. 1975. Geb.

Vol XX **Mathematische** Optimierung. Von E. Blum, W. Oettli. IX, 413 Seiten. **(daven 75 Seiten Bibliographie)**. 1975. Geb.

Vol.XXI **Stocastic Linear** Programming. By P. Kall. VI, 95 pages. 1976. Cloth.

